COP 2

917.9494
Weaver, J
PUEBLO GRANDE

Kern County Library

EL PUEBLO

GRANDE

EL PUEBLO GRANDE

A Non-Fiction Book
About Los Angeles

LOS ANGELES FROM THE BRUSH HUTS OF YANGNA TO
THE SKYSCRAPERS OF THE MODERN MEGALOPOLIS

BY JOHN D. WEAVER

THE WARD RITCHIE PRESS · LOS ANGELES

BOOKS BY JOHN D. WEAVER

Fiction
Wind Before Rain
Another Such Victory

Non-Fiction
As I Live and Breathe
The Great Experiment
Warren: The Man, The Court, The Era
The Brownsville Raid

Juvenile
Tad Lincoln: Mischief-Maker in the White House

For Harriett

Who crossed the plains in a covered Chevrolet to homestead in the Hollywood Hills (circa 1940).

Contents

*The horse, the trolley car and the automobile meet in the stately
Spring Street cañon, circa 1910.*

• I •

Spanish Colony and Mexican Capital, 1769-1849

---

*"The onward march of progress brings many
curious changes, and an old resident of the
city, returning today, would be bewildered at
the metropolitan appearance of Los Angeles."*

Los Angeles Star, May 4, 1879

The towers of the new downtown Los Angeles skyline cast long shadows across a bustling plain where an Indian village, a Spanish colonial settlement, a Mexican provincial capital and a Yankee boomtown lie buried beneath the same asphalt blanket. Civil servants and elderly derelicts, young Chicanos and middle-aged Nisei scurry through glass-and-granite canyons where long-haired aborigines once hunted antelope and bearded pioneers pruned their vineyards with the steel springs of their old beaver traps.

9

"Progress and improvement have this week laid their relentless hands upon one of the old and very familiar landmarks of the city," the *Los Angeles Star* reported a hundred years ago (September 11, 1869) when wrecking crews tore into the tile-roofed adobe mansion of the late Don José Antonio Carrillo to make way for what was to become a new Plaza landmark, the Pico House. Twenty-odd years later, when the city was creeping south on Spring and Broadway, and west on Fifth and Sixth Streets, the hotel was referred to in the public prints as "a monument of the past."

The Central City is like a schoolroom blackboard, changing from class to class. Successive waves of outlanders have attacked it with an eraser in one hand, chalk in the other, rubbing out brush huts and putting up adobe houses, leveling the adobes to make way for the red-brick shops and office buildings of Yankee entrepreneurs. The 1920's scrawled a self-portrait across the sky in the jazz moderne idiom of the black-and-gold Richfield Building. The 1970's erased it and ran up the twin 52-story towers of the Atlantic Richfield Plaza.

"The great skyscrapers of steel and terra-cotta and reinforced concrete easily crush the sun-dried walls which sheltered the simple life," a local commentator wrote in 1906, and four years later an advertisement for homes on Mount Washington ("A Real Mountain, With Real Mountain Views") pointed out that the tract was "within twenty minutes of downtown skyscrapers." Some of them had reached heights of eleven and twelve stories.

✳ ✳ ✳

"It has all the requisites for a large settlement," Fray Juan Crespi noted in his diary on August 2, 1769, when the Central City area was first viewed by civilized visitors capable of jotting down their impressions.

The Spanish explorers who had journeyed north from Mexico, or New Spain, as they preferred to call it, pitched camp on a riverbank near what is now the North Broadway entrance to Elysian Park. A delegation of about eight Indians dropped by with woven baskets as gifts. The chief brought samples of the native currency, strings of beads made of shells. "We gave them a little tobacco and glass beads," Crespi recorded, "and they went away well pleased."

As the Spaniards rode west next day along what was to become Wilshire Boulevard's Miracle Mile, they spotted "some large marshes of a certain substance like pitch; they were boiling and bubbling." Coming upon the pits of *brea* (tar) after having been jolted by half a dozen earthquakes in the last two days, the visitors wondered if this black substance had caused the temblors, but, as any child in the nearby village of Yangna could have explained, the earthquakes had been brought about by the restlessness of the seven giants whose shoulders supported the weight of the world.

In less than two hundred years the fertile river basin, dotted with clusters of brush huts, has been catapulted from the Stone Age to the Space Age. While Massachusetts militants were dumping chests of English tea into Boston harbor, the earliest known Angelenos were eating grasshoppers and running naked across what are now downtown parking lots.

Arrowheads and Angels Flight are at one with prehistoric bones, Landon buttons and Essex hubcaps, and whenever the land is laid open by earth-moving machines, reminders of earlier days keep cropping up. Excavations for the Atlantic Richfield Plaza unearthed a bed of fossiliferous material which proved to be, in effect, a page from a geological diary recording a disturbance in the downtown area some six million years ago (give or take a million), when much of the Los Angeles basin was under water. Palos Verdes was probably an island and Glendale would have been a beach town.

In the shallow water near what was to become Los Feliz Boulevard, prehistoric snails, clams and scallops were taking their ease, feeding on algae, plankton and one another, when an unheaval—perhaps an earthquake—triggered an underwater mudslide. Along with cobbles and a good part of the shellbed below them, the mollusks were swept four or five miles south to the present-day corner of Sixth and Flower, coming to rest on the bottom of the bay at a depth of about 2,000 feet, where the temperature was 42° instead of the 75° to which they had been accustomed.

In the warm coastal waters, the saturated lime solution of shell material had been in perfect balance, but once it hit the cold water, the balance was disturbed. Lime was precipitated, cementing the mollusks, rocks and shellbed in a limestone matrix. The sea animals caught up in this underwater Pompeii were still locked together in the fall of 1969 when excavators came upon a bed of fossiliferous material some sixty feet below street level.

"The biggest and best find that's ever turned up in the downtown area," said Dr. Robert Meade of the Cal State Los Angeles geology department. "I'm glad we had a chance to study it."

Most of the creatures retrieved at Sixth and Flower still flourish in local coastal waters. Somehow they managed to survive. The gentle, friendly Yangna villagers were not so fortunate. Within a hundred and fifty years of the coming of the *gente de razon* (the Spaniards were called "people of reason" to distinguish them from the natives), the aboriginal Angelenos had vanished.

✳ ✳ ✳

Although Spaniards had embarked on the conquest of Mexico in 1519, two hundred and fifty years slipped by before they ventured north into the heathen wilderness of what now constitutes the state of California. Juan Rodríguez Cabrillo sailed along its coast in 1542 and sixty years later Sebastián Vizcaíno entered San Diego Bay, but not until 1769 did the Spaniards get around to launching a land expedition north of the port of San Diego, the boundary between the sparsely settled peninsula of Baja (Lower) California and the unexplored territory of Alta (Upper) California.*

Led by the Spanish Governor of the Californias, Don Gaspar de Portolá, the expedition left San Diego July 14, heading for Monterey Bay and hoping to find suitable mission sites along the way. On August 2, the as yet undisturbed setting for downtown Los Angeles appeared to the Franciscan priest, Juan Crespi, as a "delightful place among the trees on the river." The Spaniards named the river the Porciúncula in honor of Our Lady of the Angels of Porciúncula, whose jubilee they had celebrated the day before, but usage later rechristened it the Los Angeles River.

"This plain where the river runs is very extensive," Crespi

*The two Californias were partitioned by decree of the King of Spain in 1804, with Monterey designated as the capital of Alta California.

The flat-roofed adobe village has begun to spread out toward the mountains by the 1870's.

*To still their historic fear of thirst, Angelenos store river water in a
brick reservoir in the Plaza.*

observed. "It has good land for planting all kinds of grain and seeds, and is the most suitable site of all that we have seen for a mission. . . ."

The Spaniards came back two years later and, on September 8, 1771, founded the Mission San Gabriel Arcángel about nine miles northeast of the Porciúncula River campsite. Another ten years went by before they staked out the plaza for a pueblo on the west bank of the river. The Alta California pueblos were farming communities designed to provide the food and fiber Spain's priests and soldiers needed to sustain them in their efforts to convert the "Gentiles," as the natives were called, and at the same time discourage Russia and England from encroaching on this undeveloped frontier of New Spain.

The settlers who agreed to try their luck in the Porciúncula pueblo were rounded up in the Mexican provinces of Sonora and Sinaloa. The recruiting agent had been instructed to seek out working class family men who were "healthy, robust and without known vice," because they would be "situated in the midst of a numerous population of Gentiles, docile and without malice but susceptible, like all Indians, to the first impressions of good or bad example set by the Spaniards who settle among them aiming to civilize them. . . ."

✳ ✳ ✳

On September 4, 1781, after having been quarantined about three miles south of Mission San Gabriel because of exposure to smallpox on their arduous, seven-month journey, the *vecinos pobladores* (village settlers) set out with their horses and mules to take possession of the land they had been promised. Each of the eleven family heads was entitled to a 50-by-100 foot lot facing the Plaza and to seven acres of farmland. They were also expected to share in the work of cultivating the *propios* (municipal lands) and the *realengos* (royal lands). The king's acreage would later blossom forth as Boyle Heights.

The settlers followed a dusty old Indian trail (now Mission Road), cut across a stretch of wild country destined to make way for the city of Alhambra and probably forded the Porciúncula near what was to become Aliso Street. Its name derived from the giant sycamore which a hundred years later shaded a local brewery, just as—according to legend—it had once shaded the councils of aboriginal Angelenos.

From the high ground where the Board of Education now conducts its affairs, the Indians may have watched the new people move into the neighborhood and some of the older aborigines may have recalled their first startled look at the foreigners. The *gente de razon* had been taken for gods until one of them brought down a bird with his musket. The noise had terrified the natives, but they had concluded with relief that these were not gods, because "The Giver of Life" wouldn't murder his creatures with such casual cruelty. The strangers had been dismissed as "human beings of a nasty white color, and having ugly blue eyes."

Most of the newcomers, the Indians would have noted, were dark-skinned and dark-eyed. Only two of the forty-four settlers claimed to be Spaniards. The rest were Indians, Negroes and *mestizos* (of mixed ancestry). The blood of Africa flowed in the veins of twenty-six *pobladores*. Spanish law had always made it easy for black bondsmen to buy their freedom in New Spain, and custom had raised no barriers to intermarriage.

The oldest settler was Basilio Rosas, a 67-year-old Indian who had made the difficult journey across deserts and mountains with his mulatto wife and six children. One of the boys, 12-year-old José Carlos, would later marry a native girl from Yangna (or "Yabit," as the San Gabriel missionaries called it) and long afterwards, when the pueblo celebrated the one hundred and fiftieth anniversary of its founding, their descendants in San Gabriel would have their pictures in the paper.

No eyewitness account of the pueblo's founding has ever turned up (none of the founding fathers could read and write), but myth-makers have cloaked the day's events in suitable splendor, depicting Governor Felipe de Neve on horseback at the head of a procession of priests, soldiers, settlers and converted Indians. By the start of the 20th Century the ceremony was thought to be "probably the most extensive and the most impressive that was ever held over the founding of an American city."

It is doubtful, however, that the California Governor was on hand (he hadn't shown up for the founding of San José in 1777) or that priests from Mission San Gabriel made much of a fuss over this secular intrusion on their authority. A grey-robed friar may have mumbled a blessing and the corporal in command of the three soldiers escorting the colonists may have planted the flag of Spain in the Plaza, but the *pobladores* were probably much too busy with their makeshift wickiups to bother with ceremony.

While the women fetched water from the river to cook the evening's supper, the older boys would be taking care of the livestock and the girls would be quieting baby brothers and sisters (and flirting with the soldiers). In the darkness that night, hunkering into the bare ground like savages, some of the heads of the pueblo's first families must have had misgivings about their decision to plow and plant this remote rim of Christendom the Spaniards had named *El Pueblo de la Reina de los Angeles* (The Town of the Queen of the Angels).*

* * *

On El Pueblo's fifth anniversary, when the settlers took title to their land by scratching an X on a document held out to them by the Governor's representative, José Argüello, only eight of the founding fathers were on hand. Three had been expelled as "useless." The granddaughter of one of the rejects, a 53-year-old black tailor named Luis Quintero, ended up owning a 4,500-acre ranch, Rodeo de las Aguas (Meeting of the Waters), which eventually fell into the hands of a Yankee subdivider who dubbed it Beverly Hills.

José Sinova, who had lived in Alta California for some years, joined the eight remaining settlers at the September 4, 1786 ceremony and received a deed to his land and a branding iron for his cattle. Two sons of old Basilio Rosas came of age and they, too, were granted their property rights as *pobladores*. Meanwhile, little girls were growing up and marrying young soldiers, and old frontier veterans with no homes to go back to were riding into town to live out their lives in a warm, agreeable place where there was food to eat, wine to drink and ears to bend with stories of the good old days.

*For years antiquarians have argued about the pueblo's correct title. Theodore E. Treutlein disposes of the controversy in the Spring, 1973, issue of the *Southern California Quarterly*.

During its first ten years the settlement gained twenty families, among them men with such now familiar names as Pico, Sepulveda, Figueroa and Soto. The climate was so salubrious that nine of the town's eighty adults claimed to have passed their ninetieth birthday. By the turn of the century some thirty one-story adobe houses, most of them with only a single windowless, dirt-floored room, were clustered around the Plaza, and the town was taking on the look of a retirement village for old soldiers, a few of whom had been rewarded with vast grants of land. The neighboring hills were dotted with their cattle.

Although the missionaries at San Gabriel complained of the town's preoccupation with fast horses, strong drink and loose women, the settlers managed to produce more grain, cattle, horses and sheep than any other community in Alta California. They were so far removed from the historic turmoil of the Atlantic seaboard that George Washington had been in his tomb nearly three years before they saw a ship from the United States. The arrival of the *Lelia Bird* in 1803 touched off a brisk commerce in the smuggling of otter skins and, later on, of bullock hides and tallow.

* * *

In the spring of 1822 word reached El Pueblo that Mexico had won its independence from Spain. California was now Mexican territory, with its capital remaining at Monterey. Angelenos dutifully changed the flag flying above the Plaza, replacing the Spanish lion with the Mexican serpent, and went on about their affairs. Some months later, in December, they dedicated the church it had taken them more than forty years to build. It faced the new Plaza, which had been shifted to its present location in 1818, reversing the direction of the town's growth. Instead of moving north, it had begun inching south.

Two enterprising Americanos, John Temple and George Rice, opened the town's first general merchandise store in 1828 on the southern edge of town, the site of the present Federal Building at the corner of Temple and Main. Temple bought out his partner and by 1836, according to the census figures for the Los Angeles district, he had a potential market of 2,228 customers, including the town's two hundred and fifty women, fifteen of whom were identified professionally by the initials, "M.V." (*Mala Vida*—Bad Life).

Twenty-nine of the area's fifty foreigners (other than Spaniards) hailed from the United States. Their ranks included not only Don Juan Temple but also Abel Stearns, another New England hustler. He trafficked in hides and wine, did a little smuggling on the side, and ended up as Southern California's wealthiest landowner. He was so homely his neighbors dubbed him *Cara de Caballo* (Horseface), but in 1841, at the age of 43, he picked off the city's prize beauty, his friend Juan Bandini's 14-year-old daughter, Arcadia, and installed her in an adobe mansion on what is now the southeast corner of Main and Arcadia Streets.

Thanks to José Antonio Carrillo, the hulking, swaggering plotter of revolutions who dominated Southern California politics for a quarter of a century, the town was officially declared a *ciudad* (city) in 1835 and was also designated the capital of the territory. Mexican governors, however, refused to exchange the civilized amenities of Monterey for the crudities of an overgrown village bursting with saloons, bordellos and gambling dens, but with no public buildings fit to house the government.

The raunchy reputation of the capital in name only spread to England in the 1840's when a traveler described it as a "den of thieves" teeming with "the lowest drunkards and gamblers of the country." The narrow, crooked streets meandering off from the Plaza were dusty in summer, muddy in winter, unrelieved by sidewalks or shade trees. To a disgusted local official, the gloomy, clay-colored house fronts of El Pueblo suggested "the catacombs of ancient Rome more than the habitation of a free people."

Like the Spanish explorers in the Portolá party who had been struck with wonder at the sight of the black, bubbling marshes of *brea* west of the river, 19th Century visitors were awed by the pits and impressed by the ingenious use the townspeople made of the stuff. They smeared it on their flat roofs to keep out the rain. In hot weather the tar melted and trickled down the adobe walls, forming sticky pools in the unpaved streets.

Indians were hired for a pittance to haul the *brea* in ox-drawn carts. They also made the adobe bricks, built the houses, planted the corn, crushed the grapes, ground the flour, baked the bread, cradled the babies, dug the graves, sewed the ball gowns, polished the family silver, swept the Plaza and hauled the bullock hides to San Pedro.

With native labor so cheap and abundant, Angelenos were inclined to idleness and self-indulgence, much to the disgust of the first Puritanical New Englanders to look in on them. The ladies were free to dance and flirt the night away, sleep all morning and then stroll down to Hugo Reid's new *tienda* on the Plaza to fondle a fresh shipment of silk *rebozos* from Acapulco or dining room chairs from Boston. The men never thought of walking anywhere. Even to cross the Plaza, they hopped on a horse. They were often in wine and, when the cards were running against them, in debt as well.

"In the hands of an enterprising people, what a country this might be," mused Richard Henry Dana in *Two Years Before the Mast*, an 1840 best seller. The sentiment was echoed by a Yankee trader in a letter to the folks back home: "All California wants to make it the first country of the world is about 10,000 New England farmers, with their families, churches and schools."

*　*　*

When Sir George Simpson passed through California on his 1841 trip around the world, he found its trade in the hands of foreigners, most of them from the United States. Five years later, after gringos had maneuvered Texas into the Union and California seemed manifestly destined to follow suit, an often-quoted speech attributed to Governor Pio Pico warned Californians against the "hordes of Yankee emigrants" swarming across the province.

"They are cultivating farms, establishing vineyards, erecting mills, sawing up lumber, building workshops, and doing a thousand other things which seem natural to them, but which Californians neglect or despise. What then are we to do? Shall we remain supine, while those daring strangers are overrunning our fertile plains, and gradually outnumbering and displacing us? Shall these incursions go on unchecked, until we shall become strangers in our own land?"

Pico urged secession from "the mock republic of Mexico" and annexation with France or England, the "two great powers in

Europe which seem destined to divide between them the unappropriated countries of the world." Protected by the ships and soldiers of either country, the Governor argued, Californians would once again be able to "go quietly to their ranchos, and live there as of yore, leading a merry and thoughtless life, untroubled by politics or cares of state."

Never again would Californians live so merrily and so free of political cares, and never would their guests be given quite the same hospitality. As H. H. Bancroft noted, "a person could travel from San Diego to Sonoma without a coin in his pocket, and never want for a roof to cover him, a bed to sleep on, food to eat, and even tobacco to smoke." Their hosts gave what others sold. Proud, generous, vulnerable, they were no more capable of dealing with the Yanqui's dollar than the Indians had been prepared to deal with the Spaniard's musket and cross.

Americans led by Captain John C. Frémont and Commodore Robert F. Stockton marched on Los Angeles in the summer of 1846 and entered the city August 13 without firing a shot. When they went north a few weeks later, they left an officious American officer and fifty men behind to keep an eye on the city. Rebellious Angelenos sent him packing, but four months later, on January 18, 1847, he returned with reinforcements. The Stars and Stripes went back up over the city and a band played in the Plaza while Commodore Stockton relaxed in the adobe home of Doña Encarnación Ávila on what is now Olvera Street.

"We cannot compete with the rush and complications of a civilization so unlike our own," explained an unreconstructed Californian many years later, and one of the few Indians to live to see the dawn of the 20th Century summed it up for his people in less than a dozen words: "When Indians died, the villages ended. We, all the people, ended."

*The dusty commercial establishments of South Main Street bake
in the summer sun of the 1880's.*

· II ·

Yankee Boomtown, 1850-1899

"Time, flood, and the hated gringos have long since obliterated all ancient landmarks and boundary lines of the old pueblos."

J. M. Guinn, 1895

The city fathers, staring into a bare municipal cupboard in the summer of 1840, decided to go into the real estate business, but before they could sell any part of the pueblo's Spanish land grant, an area of four square leagues (17,172.37 acres) measured "one league to each wind" from the Plaza Church, they had to have a survey of their royal patrimony. The assignment went to a 30-year-old West Pointer, Lieutenant Edward Otho Cresap Ord, grandson of George IV of England and his morganatic wife, Maria Anne Fitzherbert.

The young officer shrewdly offered to take half of his fee in land, but had to settle for cash. The *ayuntamiento* (city council) was looking ahead to the "not improbable" day when the city's population would have soared to 5,000 and the vacant lots the lieutenant had his eye on might be worth more than the $3,000 he charged for preparing the city's first map.

"We commenced last Monday," Ord's assistant, William Rich Hutton, wrote on Sunday, July 29, "& have gone from the church to the last house on main street, about 1 ¼ miles."

In the gamey native quarter north of the Plaza Church, where life was cheap and, on Saturday night, likely to end abruptly, Ord showed *Calle de Eternidad* crossing *Calle de Las Virgenes* on its way to the cemetery. For a later generation of Angelenos, Eternity Street was known as Buena Vista. It is now North Broadway. The Street of the Virgins, noted in its heyday less for its virtue than for its venery, appears on current maps as Alpine Street.

The last numbered street to the south was Eighth, but Ord's map took note of unnamed east-west streets as far out in the country as present-day Pico Boulevard. The north-south streets west of Main were *Primavera* (Spring), *Fortin* (Fort, now Broadway), *Loma* (Hill), *Aceituna* (Olive), *Caridad* (now Grand), *Esperanzas* (Hope), *Flores* (Flower) and *Calle de Los Chapules* (Street of the Grasshoppers, now Figueroa).

Grasshopper Street, at the time of the American occupation, marked the western border of the pueblo. In dry years, grasshoppers left the *cienegas* (swamps) around what is now Marina del Rey and swarmed across the parched landscape looking for vegetation to feed on. Once they came into view above *Calle de Los Chapules*, the grapegrowers knew that their vineyards in the east end of town would be devastated. They kept a wary eye on the skies above Grasshopper Street.

Ord delivered his map, or as he called it, his "Plan de La Ciudad de Los Angeles," in mid-September and the first auction was held on November 7. Fifty-four lots were sold at prices ranging from $50 to $200. Lots in the older part of town, north of the Plaza, brought less than those in the "lower district," the municipal acreage bounded by Second and Fourth, Spring and Hill. The Americans were pushing the city farther and farther away from its birthplace.

* * *

In the mining towns up north claim-jumpers and camp-followers were gorging on Southern California beef in the 1850's, while Angelenos built their first school "out in the country" on the northeast corner of Second and Spring, gulped their first oysters, imported their first bees, attended their first Protestant service and fired their first bricks in a kiln on the west side of Fort Street (Broadway) south of Second.

"But one solitary brick structure reared its walls within the precincts of the Angel city, three or four wooden tenements and the balance were adobe houses," a visiting editor noted in 1853.

As the decade drew to a close, more than thirty brick buildings went up in a single year, the most imposing of which was Abel Stearns' two-story Arcadia Block on the corner of Los Angeles and Arcadia Streets. Don Abel had also set the town's tongues to wagging by sending to Boston for the first carriage to be seen in Los Angeles. Gossips insisted the old man did it to please his young wife. Wives of lesser men still went about in *carretas*, lumbering carts mounted above two solid wheels of sawed-off logs.

Angelenos, as mirrored in the pages of the *Star*, worried about law and murder ("Crime is perpetrated openly and with impunity"), discussed the feasibility of lighting the city with gas ("Our streets will become safe and pleasant for an evening stroll"), assembled at the Mechanics' Institute to debate the question: "Should Capital Punishment Be Abolished?" and sought to preserve pedestrians as an endangered species by declaring it illegal "for any person to ride any mule, horse or other animal within the city limits at a furious rate."

"Los Angeles, prosperous, growing," Richard Henry Dana jotted down in his journal when he revisited the city in the summer of 1859.

The Mexican provincial capital had become so Americanized that it outlawed bullfighting in 1860 and formed a club "for the promotion of the manly art of base ball playing." It warmed the *Star's* Democratic, Lincoln-hating heart to see local schoolboys aping their elders by spending "their play hours in this healthy recreation." In their father's day, they would have been roping and breaking wild horses, showing off their mastery of the rawhide rope they called a *reata*.

25

The north end of town, however, held fast against change. It was still a squat, adobe Mexican village, teeming with goats, chickens and children. So many of the *paisanos* hailed from Sonora that the *barrio* was called Sonora Town. While the Plaza's landed gentry went its own aristocratic way and south side Yankees busied themselves with commerce, the men of Sonora Town found what work they could, bet on cards and cockfights, drank their one-bit wine and gave the community a reputation for drunken and often fatal quarrels.

"Last Sunday night was a brisk night for killing," reported the *Southern Californian* on March 5, 1855. "Four men were shot and several were wounded in shooting frays."

Much of the city's mayhem took place in an alley which has long since been swallowed up by the 400 block of North Los Angeles Street. One morning in 1832, so the story goes, Don José Antonio Carrillo posted a sign, *Calle de Los Negros* (Street of the Blacks) at each end of the narrow, block-long alley southeast of the Plaza owned and occupied by Los Negros, as all dark-skinned Angelenos were called at that time.

The name stuck for more than forty years, but in common usage the 500-foot strip of adobe brothels, saloons and tenements was referred to as Negro, or more often, Nigger Alley. In a community which has never been known to back off from the use of a superlative, it was called "the wickedest street on earth." At one time it was averaging a homicide a day, not counting Indians.

The criminal violence of Nigger Alley was as effective as a firing squad in destroying the descendants of the aboriginal Angelenos. After the missions were reduced to the status of parish churches by secularization in the 1830's, the Indians had found themselves in a cultural limbo, cut off from the institutionalized life of the missions, unable to go back to their old ways or to cope with the new. They had turned to thievery and prostitution to support their addiction to *aguardiente*, a raw native brandy which served as a blindfold while their unpronounced sentence of death was being carried out.

"The brute upshot of missionization, in spite of its kindly flavor and humanitarian roots," A. L. Kroeber observed, "was only one thing: death."

From Fort Moore Hill oldtimers watch the Yankee city move south, farther and farther from its Plaza birthplace.

*In the native quarter north of the Plaza, shaded by pepper trees,
Sonora Town holds out against change.*

On Christmas Eve, 1861, it started to rain and, with two slight interruptions, it lasted for thirty days. The city's new public water system collapsed. Adobe walls crumbled. Vineyards and orchards were swept away. Firewood stacked in the cañons was carried out to sea. Main Street shopkeepers stood in water waist-deep, struggling to save their merchandise.

By spring, however, the weather was delightful and, the *News* observed, the hills were "covered with a luxuriant growth of grass." Having dug themselves out from the mud and debris, Angelenos took up football, built a brick sewer, argued slavery and secession, and suddenly found themselves up against a small-pox epidemic. It started among the Indians in November, 1862, and spread quickly, taking a particularly cruel toll in Sonora Town. Yellow flags marked the stricken adobes and deaths were so frequent that the city fathers put a stop to ringing the Plaza Church bells for the souls of the departed.

A curse seemed to have been laid upon the land when the plague, in 1864, gave way to drought, and lean, long-horned cattle were staggering across the lion-colored hills, dying in dusty creekbeds. Finally, in mid-November, 1865, the rains returned and the *News* rejoiced at the beauty of the countryside ("one vast meadow"). With the end of the drought came the end of the pastoral age. The rancheros had been done in by depressed cattle prices, withered grass, delinquent tax bills and unpaid loans.

The gracious, hospitable Dons had never given much thought to maps and documents establishing ownership of land that everybody knew was theirs until they had to defend their Spanish and Mexican grants in Yanqui courts. They were incapable of coping with the gringo's legalisms (not to mention the interest rates on what many of them had taken to be a neighbor's friendly loan). Their day was done; the day of the developer was at hand.

"Many of the largest grants of land in the county have been subdivided and thrown into market," the *News* reported in 1868, and six years later the *Star* beamed approvingly at the disappearance of the city's adobe houses, which "do well enough for a country where all out of doors is not considered too much for a melon-patch, but in a community of Anglo-Saxons, where men institute expensive lawsuits to establish the right to possession and ownership of three inches, or even one inch, of frontage, walls two or three feet thick 'won't pay.' "

* * *

On the epoch-making spring day of May 10, 1869, when San Francisco was linked with the eastern seaboard by the golden spike driven into the ground at Promontory Point, Utah, to mark completion of the country's first transcontinental railroad, Angelenos were still depending on horses, mules and oxen to carry their guests and their grapes, wine, oranges, lemons, grain and wool between the city and its port, but Phineas Banning, whose stage-coaches and freight wagons had been making the Los Angeles-San Pedro run for years, was about to propel the community's archaic transportation industry into the nineteenth century.

After getting himself elected to the State Senate, he pushed through two railroad bills authorizing the county and city of Los Angeles to subscribe $225,000 in capital stock. The bills were signed by the Governor on February 1, 1868. The scheme would bankrupt local government, diehards insisted, but when the proposal was placed on the ballot the following month, a majority of the electorate opted for the railroad. Developers tumbled over one another bidding up the price of urban real estate.

"During the past week," the *News* reported, "land situated two miles from the Plaza sold for $80 per acre that could have been bought one year ago for $14 per acre. Nearer the business center, lots one hundred and twenty feet front are now selling for $1,000 which could be purchased three months ago for $300."

The first railroad south of the Tehachapis formally opened on the morning of October 26, 1869. A train left the new Los Angeles depot on the southwest corner of Alameda and Commercial Streets at nine o'clock and pulled into Wilmington within the hour. The harbor area depot was located on a fifteen-acre tract Senator Banning had parted with for a consideration of $39,000. The Senator had also won the contract to build the tracks at a cost of $19,000 per mile.

* * *

When Spain staked its claim to California, the king's priests and soldiers built a string of missions and presidios along a royal highway. When the Southern Pacific staked its claim to the state a hundred years later, it built a string of railroad depots* designed not only to accommodate passengers and freight, but also to remind the town that it owed its prosperity, perhaps even its existence, to what Californians called "The Octopus."

The Octopus wriggled south from San Francisco, gathering farm towns into its steel tentacles. If a town resisted its demands, it was denied rail service, and then left to wither and die. While SP construction crews ran up new depots in the center of towns willing to knuckle under, SP land agents were fanning out over the San Joaquin Valley creating such communities as Modesto, Merced and Fresno. When The Octopus crawled to the Tehachapis, it paused, giving Los Angeles time to consider its terms.

Along with the usual right-of-way, it demanded a chunk of cash, sixty acres in the middle of the city for a depot and control of the Los Angeles & San Pedro Railroad. Angelenos fumed for a year and finally, in 1872, gave in. Four years later, on September 5, the San Francisco-to-Los Angeles track was joined at Lang's Station in Soledad Cañon near Newhall.

The Octopus also took over the Los Angeles & Independence Railroad, which carried young lovers out to the beach at Santa Monica and gave local merchants, manufacturers, farmers and winegrowers a harbor closer to San Francisco than San Pedro. Once it acquired the line, the SP razed its wooden depot on San Pedro Street. The entrance had been flanked by the two bronze sphinxes pictured in contemporary annals as being "of heroic size and rather imposing demeanor." They disappeared for a while, only to be resurrected in the front yard of Cora Phillips' sporting house on Alameda Street, a block or so south of the SP depot.

$$* \quad * \quad *$$

With the completion of the transcontinental railroad, the state's labor market was overrun by Chinese, many of whom had originally come to California in search of gold. While politicians com-

---

*"*Depot* is very commonly used instead of station, and in many places the latter word, when used alone, means police-station."—*Baedeker's United States,* 1909.

peted for the workingman's vote by trying to outdo one another in trumpeting their dislike and distrust of the "heathen Chinee," some of the Orientals drifted away from the industrial north to the agricultural south, where they were not competing with Caucasians when they opened wash-houses in Los Angeles, peddled vegetables and gradually ousted Indians and Negroes from suburban kitchens.

By 1870 there were one hundred and seventy-two Chinese in the city, dozens of them concentrated in the adobe hovels of Nigger Alley where, on the evening of October 26, 1871, a white man stopped a Chinese bullet while trying to help a policeman break up an altercation between two rival tongs. The death of Robert Thompson in a Main Street drug store touched off a five-hour orgy of shooting, stabbing, hanging and looting that left nineteen Chinese dead.

Next morning when the bodies were laid out in double rows on the northern side of the jail, where City Hall now stands, rope still trailed from some of the broken necks. The mob had torn the trousers from the body of Chinatown's highly respected doctor, Chee Long Tong, to get at the money in his pockets and had hacked the ring finger from another corpse. With one exception, eyewitnesses told a newspaper reporter, none of the dead men had been guilty of any wrongdoing.

The November term grand jury called 111 witnesses, most of whom showed "a blamable reluctance" to tell what they knew of the "crimes which must cause christianity to weep, civilization to blush, and humanity to mourn." The jurors came to the "painful conclusion" that law enforcement officers had been "deplorably inefficient," having made no attempt "to arrest any of those, who, in their presence were openly, and grossly, violating the law, even to the taking of human life."

The evidence suggested to the jurors that "a great majority of those who witnessed the sad spectacles of that night, instead of being a blood-thirsty mob, having possession of the city, or any part of it, trampling law and order under foot, were unwilling witnesses, anxious to prevent the revolting scenes that were passing before their eyes and would, quickly and cheerfully, have prevented, or put an end to the anarchy, if any resolute and ener-

Parking becomes a problem in the business center, where Spring and Main Streets meet at Temple.

Cable cars stand ready to whisk the sheep to the fleecing areas.

getic man, clothed with authority, and with an average share of ability and judgment, had placed himself at their head, and in a proper manner directed their efforts."

Many of the defendants, seeking to justify their criminal conduct, testified that they had merely carried out orders given them by law enforcement officers on the scene. "There is ground to suspect that improper instructions were given by officers," the grand jury report acknowledged, but nearly a hundred years before the Nuremberg trials and the My Lai massacre, the jurors pointed out that "the orders of an officer are no excuse for the commission of a criminal act."

"The jury handed in forty-nine indictments, twenty-five of which are for the crime of murder and accessories," the *Star* reported.* Seven men were found guilty and given sentences of from two to six years. The judge who presided over the trials was Robert M. Widney, one of the founders of the University of Southern California. Recently appointed to fill a vacancy on the bench, Judge Widney was not sufficiently steeped in the law's subtleties to spot a fatal defect in the indictments. The convictions were reversed on appeal and the seven men set free.

Under a shameful state law, Chinese were not permitted to testify in matters involving Caucasians at the time of the Nigger Alley massacre. The law was quietly done away with in 1873, however, and a covey of Chinese merchants promptly sued the city for its negligence in permitting a mob to pillage their shops. The grand jury, it would appear, had paved the way for the plaintiffs by calling attention to the deplorable inefficiency of local authorities, but the inscrutable Occidentals sitting on the state's highest tribunal ruled against the Chinese merchants because of their failure "to summon the police before the shooting commenced."

✳ ✳ ✳

Easterners discovered Los Angeles in 1871 when its slaughter of the Chinese hit the front pages of their newspapers and its grapes

*In accounts of the Chinese Massacre, the number of indictments varies widely. Paul M. DeFalla's study of the case led him to conclude that twenty-three men were indicted, but two were never brought to court.

went on exhibit at their state fairs ("grown under glass," snorted the disbelievers). Not knowing quite what to make of this blood-stained Eden, the venturesome travelers from the Atlantic seaboard who turned up at the Pico House clutching Spanish phrasebooks were agreeably surprised to find gas lamps and running water. John Moore, the *Star* announced, was planning to open a restaurant "on the San Francisco plan—everything to be sold by the plate."

The pueblo, in its nineties now, was trying to live down its past. "Just think of it!" the *Star* crowed at the start of 1873. "Only two drunks arrested on New Year's Day. Talk about your moral cities." The editor worried about changing mores ("The girls nowadays wear false hair, paint and—heaven knows what they won't do"), poked fun at the new blue laws ("A man may kiss his wife in his own house between two and four o'clock on Sunday morning") and grunted approval of the board of education's decisions to start expelling any youngster who came to school packing a firearm.

Visitors picked and ate a fresh orange, admired the Plaza's new fountain (a boy with a dolphin), traipsed through the east-side vineyards, made a brave stab at the Mexican cuisine, cooled their throats with the local beer, returned from a day's outing at Santa Monica clutching an abalone shell and, at dusk, watched the city's lamplighter ride through the streets from lamp to lamp. They shuddered at the filthy canals from which the city drank and were amused, outraged or delighted when they stumbled into what they mistook for genteel boarding houses.

"There is a small street running almost parallel with and not more than a hundred blocks distant from Los Angeles Street," the *Star* noted. "There are a number of small frame houses on this thoroughfare, apparently very desirable places of residence. A stranger is looking for a house wherein to sojourn while in the city. He wants a room on some quiet street away from the bustle and noise of the business locality. He is struck with the calm and secluded appearance of the houses on this street. If he can only procure lodging here it will just suit him. While thus reflecting, lo! and behold! the wished for sign 'Furnished Rooms' meets his gaze.

36

"He opens the gate and walking to the door, knocks. A bashful maiden opens it, and he makes known his business. She asks him to walk in and take a seat in the parlor, while she goes to inform her 'ma.' This he does, and after waiting a few moments he is confronted by a virtuous-looking elderly female. He tells her he would like to obtain a room, and is mortified and dumbfounded with virtuous indignation when she asks him if he wishes it 'with or without ladies?' He is in a house of shame."

The city's guests went home remembering the gamecocks in the native quarter, the Chinese vegetable peddlers, the sixteen-mule teams lumbering along Los Angeles Street, the farm wagons parked around the Plaza, the new cottages clinging to the scarred cliffs in the west end and the stench of sewage so overpowering in some areas—Sixth and Main, for one—that windows couldn't be opened on hot afternoons.

On one such afternoon in September, 1872, the editor of the *Star* scrambled to the top of Telegraph Hill and, mopping his brow, looked down at the "gallant little place." His admiring gaze came to rest on the new City Park (Pershing Square). Just across the way, on Sixth Street west of Fort (Broadway), where an alleyway now provides a side-door entrance to the Los Angeles Theater, stood the front of St. Vincent's College. It was located, a guidebook noted, in "a pleasant, retired part of the city."

"Great hotels will be built in the vicinity of St. Vincent's College," the editor predicted, "and there will be the heart of the city."

✳   ✳   ✳

In the 1870's, tourists came to see the city. In the 1880's settlers came to stay. They wept over *Ramona*, rode the new cable cars, watched the orange groves at Fifth and Charity (Grand) give way to the State Normal School, spoke for the first time on a telephone, thrilled to the introduction of electric lights and, in 1889, changed the historic name of Fort Street to Broadway. The street had been named for Fort Moore, where, on July 4, 1847, the United States flag had been raised above the Mexican capital and the townspeople had listened to the luminous words of Señor Jefferson's Declaration of Independence read aloud in English and Spanish.

37

The newcomers swept aside the city's cultural heritage. They named their streets after Yankee subdividers rather than Spanish explorers or Mexican colonists. Most of the old names had been obliterated by 1897 when a citizen's committee was appointed to systematize the city's street names. The committee recommended the use of "many Spanish titles, taking care that they shall be appropriate, musical, not too long, and not easily mispronounced."

The City Council agreed to the recommendations, but they were turned down by the mayor. He was afraid the names might "prove very troublesome to newcomers from the East." Among the offending names he cited were Alcantara, Arapahoe, Cerro Gordo, Cimarron, Juanita and Montecito. The city's history had faded so far from memory that a street named for a Mexican governor, Micheltorena, was thought to honor a forgotten Irishman, one Michael Torrance.

✳   ✳   ✳

During the 1890's Angelenos got their first look at the horseless carriage, read a prediction that someday the human voice would be transmitted to other planets, listened to warnings from the newly formed Sierra Club ("If we denude our forests, there will be trouble ahead for us"), trooped into Athletic Park to watch the Boston Bloomer Girls play baseball (the home team was made up of theater employees) and clapped a half-hour parking limit on horses hitched in the downtown area.

The completion of the $70,000 Hellman Building at Second and Broadway in 1897 would "contribute to the retention of the business center where it now is, retarding the southerly march of business houses," the *Times* announced, standing bravely against the tide sweeping the city south. Business had been moving in that direction for two generations, ever since John Temple opened his store on the street that bears his name.

The city had been given another southerly shove in the 1880's when Remi Nadeau chose the First and Spring Streets corner now occupied by the *Times* as the site for a grand hotel. It was the first four-story building to pierce the downtown skyline and the first to boast a passenger elevator. The action shifted from the Nadeau to the Van Nuys when it opened its doors at Fourth and Main in January, 1897.

"A neat device for the electrical heating of curling irons in each room is a new feature of special interest to ladies," the *Times* reported.

Eastern travel agents were vying with one another for the most seductive package deal on Southern California excursions. One outfit built a grand hotel in Pasadena and offered its patrons the convenience of traveling "from Boston to the hotel elevator without change of car, and with coupons to pay all their expenses *en route*." A competitor advertised personally conducted tours for sybarites who would not only enjoy the comforts of three drawing room-sleeping cars, but also "a barber shop, bath rooms for ladies and gentlemen, library, grand piano, a stenographer and typewriter, a chaperone and ladies' maid."

Meanwhile, the *Times* was boasting about the city's new buildings ("a magnificent courthouse, a city hall and a high school"), its public library ("excites the envy and surprise of other cities"), its two handsome theaters, Grand Opera House and Hazard's Pavilion ("a first-class show will always draw a full house in Los Angeles"), its high-masted electric street lamps ("the lights are visible by mariners many miles out at sea") and its up-to-date system of street railways ("the cables all make a speed of 8½ miles per hour, and the horse lines 7½ miles per hour").

The city now extended three miles, instead of two and a half, in each direction from the Plaza. East Los Angeles had become "one of the most beautiful residence sections" and Boyle Heights was "rapidly settling up." At the height of the great boom (1886-88), there had not been a foot of paved street in the city. When Angelenos took inventory on New Year's Day, 1891, they counted 87 miles of paved streets and 78 miles of cement sidewalks. A modern city had sprung up in the last decade, and with its fivefold increase in population (up from 11,311 to 50,394) had come congestion and pollution.

Park commissioners were frantically looking about for open space. "There has, until recently, been so much open ground in all directions within half a mile of the city center that the need of breathing places has not been felt," the *Times* pointed out.

Growth had also given rise to fears for the environment. The city engineer was under pressure to devise an effective sewerage system to replace the controversial proposal to carry the main outfall from the southeast corner of the city to the sea ("one of the leading objections to the previous plan was the anticipated pollution of the ocean beach near Santa Monica").

The Plaza, as it looked to the visitors who showed up at the Pico House in the 1870's, practicing their phrase-book Spanish.

· III ·
Oil and Water, 1900-1910

"*The northern half of California is the seat*
of a relatively old and stable civilization.
It has a tradition of good living. Its
principal city, San Francisco, is one of the
most charming and romantic of American towns ...
In Southern California there is no such
charm and no such tradition."

H. L. Mencken, 1927

Easterners paying their first visit to the west coast around the turn of the century found themselves exploring two Californias. Although statehood forced them to share a common legislative domicile in Sacramento, they lived apart, one in name only. San Francisco, the liberal, worldly, Catholic, trade unionist capital of the north, went in for fine wines and elegant restaurants. South of the Tehachapi Mountains, conservative, provincial, Protestant, open shop Angelenos made do with meatloaf and buttermilk, secure in the knowledge that temperance and industry would be rewarded with prosperity in this world, salvation in the next.

The comfortable working relationship between Angelenos and their Maker (the sort of deity a man could put up for membership in the California Club) was reflected in the message General Harrison Gray Otis, publisher of the *Times*, cabled his staff from Yokohama in December, 1906, when the paper was about to celebrate its first twenty-five years of publication:

HOMEWARD BOUND. GRATEFUL FOR ESCAPE FROM OVERMASTERING DISEASE. CONGRATULATIONS ON OUR ANNIVERSARY. REVIEWING SURPASSING ACHIEVEMENTS AND RICH BLESSINGS IN THE PAST QUARTER CENTURY, I REVERENTLY EXCLAIM: "LORD, GOD OF HOSTS, BE WITH US YET, LEST WE FORGET, LEST WE FORGET."

San Francisco, with its port facilities, railway terminals, banks and factories, seemed obviously destined to be the commercial, financial and industrial capital of the American West until the powerful downtown Angelenos who were looking after the city's best interests and their own as well decided the time had come to see that the pueblo acquired what an otherwise bountiful providence had neglected to supply. They set out to dredge a deepwater harbor and build an aqueduct.

The harbor project pitted General Otis against Collis P. Huntington, president of the Southern Pacific, in a battle for federal funds. The money should go into harbor improvements at San Pedro, the *Times* insisted. The Octopus, eager to control the city's waterfront traffic (and the city as well, of course), fought for a port at Santa Monica. The San Pedro forces organized what they called the Free Harbor League and, with the help of Stephen M. White in the United States Senate, managed to derail the Southern Pacific.

Work on the San Pedro breakwater began April 26, 1899, accompanied by suitable oratory, band music and a barbecue. It was finished in 1910. The task of dredging the inner harbor was well along by the time the Panama Canal opened four years later. San Diego and San Francisco, with their splendid natural harbors, found themselves sharing the world's maritime commerce with an inland city.

In the meantime, the city fathers had resorted to some artful gerrymandering. First, in 1906, they had annexed a "shoestring strip" which gave the city a corridor from its southern limits to the San Pedro-Wilmington area. Under state law, however, one incorporated city could not annex another, so Angelenos got the law changed to permit "consolidation." In August, 1909, San Pedro and Wilmington agreed to be consolidated, and the pueblo became a seaport city.

As the population shot past the 100,000-mark in 1900, the city saw itself hurtling toward the dread day when it would have to increase its supply of water or decrease its supply of settlers. With limitless growth a basic tenet of their booster faith ("Big is Good, Bigger is Better, Biggest is Best"), Angelenos began to cast about for new sources of water. They had enough to slake the thirst of about 250,000 residents. They were then thinking in terms of 2,000,000.

Fred Eaton, an engineer and a former mayor (1898-1900), had explored the possibility of building an aqueduct to tap the melted snow flowing from the eastern slopes of the Sierra Nevada into the Owens River some two hundred and fifty miles north of Los Angeles. He persuaded William Mulholland, the municipal water department's superintendent and chief engineer, to look into his scheme. Eaton also had the foresight to file a claim in his own name for much of the river's surplus flow and for land which could be used for dams and reservoirs.

After rattling across the path of the proposed aqueduct in a mule-drawn buckboard, Mulholland pronounced the project feasible and put a price tag on it of something in the neighborhood of $24,500,000. In July, 1905, General Otis sprang it on his readers (TITANIC PROJECT TO GIVE CITY A RIVER). Two months later the city's voters approved a $1,500,000 bond issue to acquire Owens Valley lands and water rights, including the Eaton options. An additional bond issue of of $23,000,000 was passed in 1907 and work began on what the press called "The Panama Canal of the West."

No American city had ever faced such an engineering chal-

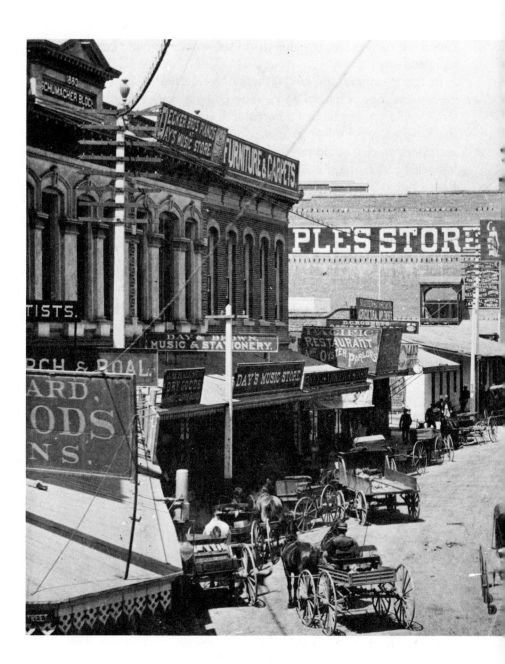

Double-parking, a Spring Street nuisance at the turn of the century.

lenge. The 233-mile aqueduct had to pass over foothills, through mountains (its 142 separate tunnels totalled 52 miles) and across the Mojave Desert. But before Mulholland's 5,000-man army could lay a foot of conduit, a 120-mile railroad had to be built to carry heavy machinery into the northern wilderness. Construction crews could be supplied only by building 500 miles of highway and trails which were buried at times by blizzards and sandstorms. Finally, on November 5, 1913, some 40,000 Angelenos turned out to watch the Owens River water cascade into a San Fernando Valley reservoir.

"There it is," said Mulholland, "take it."

Two groups of land speculators were also waiting to take it. The San Fernando Mission Land Company had picked up 16,000 acres of valley land in 1904 with a view to making a profit if and when Henry E. Huntington* ran trolley tracks out from the city. The other syndicate, the Los Angeles Homes Company, representing the interests of General Otis and his son-in-law, Harry Chandler, had acquired some 47,500 acres in 1909-10, counting on the Owens Valley water to enable them to turn a handsome profit.

The water belonged to the city's taxpayers who had put up the money to fetch it from the High Sierra. Before it could be siphoned off to irrigate the San Fernando Valley holdings of the speculators, the city had to go through the formality of annexation. On May 4, 1915, voters obligingly agreed to cram 168 square miles of farming land into the city's borders.

Sale of water to valley ranchers would lower their taxes, they thought. Instead, their taxes went up to pay for the cost of extending city services to such a vast, sparsely settled territory. The San Fernando Valley annexation (Palms was picked up the same day) boosted the city's total area to 280 square miles, exactly ten times the size of the pueblo's land grant from the King of Spain.

✳ ✳ ✳

Something deep in the municipal genes has always stirred uneasily at the sight of undisturbed land. In its infancy, the settlement's

---

*Not to be confused with his Uncle Collis who led and lost the fight against the Free Harbor League.

survival depended on clearing and cultivating the surrounding wilderness. In later years, the pueblo came to regard a stand of cottonwoods or a chaparral covered hillside as a reproach, like the memory of a childhood scolding for having left food on a plate while less fortunate youngsters were going to bed hungry.

"The cottages which are being erected by Mr. Beaudry along the hillside on Fort Street are certainly a very great improvement in that part of town," the *Star* reported in 1870, nearly twenty years before Yankee boosters changed the street's name to Broadway. "Here was a bare and barren hillside, presenting a very repulsive prospect to the beholder."

The owners of Prudent Beaudry's cottages, the editor was happy to add, would be supplied with "all the requisites of water and gas." In short, by taxing Mr. Beaudry's neighbors to pay for the municipal services to be provided purchasers of his viewsite homes, the city had started subsidizing the mutilation of its hills.

"The portion of the city which might be most beautiful and picturesque—all that northern section with its chain of rolling hills —is being utterly ruined through the mistaken greed and ignorance of real estate speculators," the Municipal Art Commission reported in 1909. "With the exception of a very few tracts, on which are laid out beautiful and winding roads that follow the contour, there is a ruthless slashing into hillsides. . . ."

In City Hall, where councilman were chosen, the *Star* observed in 1860, "from 'good fellows' and 'best citizens,' " it was an article of faith that raw land should be taken away from the mule deer and turned over to men of their sort who could be counted on to do something with it. Mr. Beaudry was one of the "good fellows" and "best citizens" who dutifully took his turn serving as a city councilman and as mayor.

In their eagerness to dispose of the four square leagues of pueblo lands handed down from the Spaniards, the American city fathers gave away 35-acre "donation lots" in the 1850's to anyone who would spend $200 on improvements within a 12-month period. Inevitably, the gifts had come back to haunt City Hall in the form of petitions for schools, streets, sewers, water and lights, along with demands for the protective services of the police and fire departments.

47

"There yet remain a few acres of domain to the city out of tens of thousands, her original heritage," the Mayor reported to the Council as the 1860's drew to a close. "Protect this by every advisable barrier, keep it out of the grasp of the grabber, sharper and speculator."

But the city ran through its royal patrimony like a wastrel prince, flinging away its grandchildren's parks and playgrounds so recklessly that by 1891 the 450 acres of Elysian Park accounted for four-fifths of all the land in the municipal park system. The city fathers had managed to hold onto this last sizeable remnant of their 17,172-acre legacy only because of their inability to give it away, much less sell it.

*　*　*

Henry E. Huntington left San Francisco in 1902 and moved to Los Angeles, determined to "join this whole region in one big family." A generation of Angelenos rode his red (interurban) and yellow (local) trolley cars to the office, the theater, the beach and the mountains. Racing along at speeds of forty and fifty miles an hour (the horse car had moved at the rate of seven and one-half miles an hour), the Pacific Electric cars enabled Southern Californians to live among orange trees and work in downtown skyscrapers.

"Los Angeles is a busy centre for short trips, chiefly made now by electric cars," *Baedeker's United States* informed travelers in 1909.

The local fare was five cents. It cost fifteen cents to make the half-hour trip to Pasadena ("a thriving business city and health resort"). The hour-long, fifty-cent journey to Santa Monica took tourists through Hollywood ("a suburb of charming homes"), and could be extended to Venice ("with canals, etc., in imitation of its European namesake"). For a dollar, the big spenders could travel a hundred miles along the Pacific Electric's "Great Surf Route," which included not only Long Beach ("a frequented summer resort, with 2,250 inhab.") and San Pedro ("the National Government is now constructing a huge breakwater here"), but also Compton ("the centre of the dairy district").

In the first decade of the new century, as Pacific Electric tracks

A massive display of force by the city's mounted constabulary in the early years of the new century.

Broadway, near Second, as it appeared about the time a couple of tinkerers put together the city's first horseless carriage.

snaked across the countryside, the population of Los Angeles tripled (from 102,479 to 319,198). Long Beach shot up from 2,252 to 17,809, Santa Monica from 3,057 to 7,847, Redondo Beach from 855 to 2,935 and Burbank from 3,048 to 12,255.

"City making now is different from that of previous times," the editor of the *Express* pointed out on a fall day in 1905, shortly after Angelenos had agreed to go along with the acquisition of Owens Valley water rights. "Modern transportation methods make it possible to weave into a harmonious unit a larger section than was possible until late years."

Even if Greater Los Angeles stretched out twenty-five miles to both the northwest and the southeast, as seemed probable, a commuter would still be able to pick a fresh boutonniere from his garden, catch an interurban electric car and reach his downtown office within an hour. Warming to the message of his tea leaves, the editor went on to describe a future city which would serve as "the world's symbol of all that is beautiful and healthful and inspiring."

"It will retain the flowers and orchards and lawns, the invigorating free air from the ocean, the bright sunshine and the elbow room, which have marked it as peculiar in the past and which now are secured for all time by the abundance of the water supply. It will not become congested like the older cities, for the transportation lines, built in advance of the demands, have made it possible to get far out in the midst of the orchards and fields for home making."

The pattern for the city's sprawling development had been established by the world's finest mass rapid transit system. No one foresaw its doom when, at two o'clock on a May morning in 1897, a pair of tinkerers rolled a four-cylinder horseless carriage out of a West Fifth Street shop and took a few friends on a trial spin through the business district.

"One fear which had been felt beforehand was that the machine would scare horses, because of its unique appearance and because of the noise of the gasoline motors and the gasoline explosions," the *Times* reported. "A number of teams were passed during the trial trip, but they showed not the slightest fear of the novel spectacle."

At the time the city's first gasoline-powered tallyho rattled past mule teams on Main Street, some five hundred wells were pumping oil in an area roughly bounded by Figueroa, First, Union and Temple. The oil boom had been launched by Edward L. Doheny in November, 1892, with a well dug near the present intersection of Second Street and Glendale Boulevard.

"This is one of the leading industries of the city, and all legislation bearing on it should be liberal," warned the incoming Mayor in January, 1897, when the City Council was working on an ordinance forbidding drilling operations near city parks.

Angelenos, caught up in the Black Gold Rush of the 1890's, were living above a supply so abundant that, as the *News* had pointed out in 1865, "whole tracts of land are found in this region which cannot be traversed on foot, in consequence of the thick coating of soft 'tar.' " The tar, or *brea* as the oldtimers called it, was congealed petroleum.

The Indians had used it to caulk their boats and waterproof their woven baskets. The *gente de razon* had covered their roofs with it to ward off the winter rains. It was still keeping Angelenos dry on January 24, 1865 when a group of their wealthy neighbors got together and formed the Pioneer Oil Company "for the purpose of prospecting for petroleum." It was to be used to light lamps and grease axles. Three weeks later the editor of the *News* drove out to the "city *brea* lands" to look in on the wildcatters.

"It will be no small astonishment to our citizens to find that incalcuable fortunes lie in the very substance with which, as many of them believe, they have been 'sorely afflicted;' that which they have 'scraped from their shoes' for three-quarters of a century past," the editor wrote, and one Saturday evening the following March he conducted an experiment.

He stopped by the Main Street "oil headquarters" of Sackett & Morgan and bought four ounces of locally produced coal oil (or "kerosine," as some called it). He poured the sample into one of the lamps used for setting type and filled another lamp with eastern coal oil. The local product ignited more readily, burned more brightly ("without the slightest wavering") and left no crust on the wick.

The towering masts of the city's street lighting system are a familiar sight for Boyle Heights commuters.

One of the Victorian showplaces of the prospering city.

"We can produce an article of oil in abundance, which is equal, if not vastly superior to anything of the kind now held in the market," the editor declared, and before autumn had run its course guests at the Bella Union Hotel were dining by the light of "a fine quality of refined coal oil" from a San Fernando Valley refinery.

The California product, however, failed to live up to the hopes of its backers or the testimonial of the *News* editor. Refiners didn't know how to cope with raw material which contained less paraffin and more carbon than eastern crude oil. As a result, the lubricating oils were more watery than those from back east, and the kerosine more likely to blacken lamp chimneys with smoke. Even worse, the local oils were usually more expensive. Some seventy oil companies sprang up during California's shortlived boom. When it collapsed in 1867, all save one went under.

"The employment of petroleum, and the various preparations made from it, is becoming very general throughout the world, superseding candles, whale, palm, and other oils for illuminating as well as lubricating purposes and generating steam," the *Daily News* editorialized in the spring of 1872, and the following June the *Star* insisted that unless "our entire population are fools," Angelenos should establish an oil refinery and get on with the business of "developing our oil region into one of the most extensive and valuable properties in the United States."

In the 1890's, when California ranked as the country's third oil-producing state (behind Pennsylvania and New York), Los Angeles emerged as the oil capital of the West. Wildcatters watched the price of crude shoot up from $1.20 to $1.80 a barrel in 1900, and a few years later sink to fifteen cents. The automobile, with its insatiable thirst for petroleum products, was still a rich man's plaything.

Natural gas usually shows up wherever crude oil is found, and back in the 1870's an enterprising outfit had peddled illuminating gas from Ventura County to northern Californians with the sales pitch that it was "superior to coal gas in light and purity, and moves through the meters less swiftly," but for years California oil companies continued to rid themselves of the nuisance by burning it in the field.

Oil and gas came to mind when William Andrew Spalding,

55

reminiscing about the city's mood at the turn of the century, commented on the unfailing cheerfulness of Angelenos in the face of adversity. They had seen their cattle die, their banks fail and their real estate boom collapse; they had survived earthquakes, fires, floods and the Southern Pacific, and always they had "come up smiling after each throw-down" and gone on with the business of building a metropolis.

"When an oil belt was developed within the city boundaries which seemed to bring as much destruction of values as it produced—when there was no system, no order—when oil went to waste and the gas escaped—when there was no market for the product, and the price fell to ten cents a barrel—then the people addressed themselves to solving the strange problem, this embarrassment of riches.

"They constructed storage tanks, and devised means of transportation; they invented burners, and learned how to use crude oil for steam generation and brick-making; they learned how to utilize the crude oil in road making; they acquired the art and devised the apparatus for refining; they discovered a way for saving and utilizing the gas that had been escaping from their wells; they prospected with 'wild-cat' boring until they had extended the territory miles outside the originally developed area. In short, they established one of the greatest petroleum fields in the world. With such a record of courage, persistence and achievement, it is no wonder that Los Angeles began the new century with a stout heart and a confident air."

✳ ✳ ✳

Fifty thousand spectators showed up on January 1, 1900 for Pasadena's eleventh annual Tournament of Roses. "Every train and every electric car was crammed," the *Times* reported, and noted that every available tallyho, coach and rig within a twenty-mile radius of Orange Grove Boulevard was also pressed into service. While waiting for the parade to pass by, Angelenos read about the Boers in South Africa (they were losing their war) and the Americans in the Philippines (they were winning).

A 1900 Yale Bicycle was available for $35 ("We sell on installments") and, for $5, "a full set of teeth on rubber." Hypochondriacs could load up on cod liver oil ("the standard remedy for lung trouble") and, depending on sex, Ajax tablets ("Made Me a Man") or French Female Pills. They could also apply to an Oriental Seer who was prepared to give "valuable advice concerning all matters of health, obscure or nervous disease, evil habits and weaknesses of men and women." If all else failed, a bottle of eight-year-old Plantation Whiskey could be had for seventy-five cents.

The Mayor was concerned about the size of the police force ("totally inadequate") and the City Council with its refusal to enforce a new ordinance regulating the height of billboards. "If the chair had the authority," declared the council president, "he would take every officer on the police force and chop down all the billboards in the city." H. Gaylord Wilshire, a flamboyant Socialist who enjoyed a monopoly on billboards at the time, countered with the remark that they "soothed and satisfied the esthetic sense."*

Visually, the city was suffering the modern blight of billboards, light standards and power lines, but morally it had undergone a reformation at the hands of the white Anglo-Saxon Protestants who had defected during the boom years from county seat law offices, drug stores, dairy barns, funeral parlors and Baptist parsonages. They had proceeded to rip the vine leaves from the pueblo's hair and turn a Latin carnival into a midwestern covered dish supper. In their efforts to keep their neighbors from pleasuring themselves, especially on Sunday, they made life miserable for the three councilmen who, in the late 1890's, served on the City Council's Committee on Public Morals.

The committee was badgered with demands for ordinances restraining hotels and restaurants from selling cigars on Sunday and prohibiting anyone under the age of fifteen from being "on the streets, alleys or public places of the City of Los Angeles at night after nine o'clock." They sought to outlaw "the exhibition of photographic or kinetoscopic pictures representing prize fights" and when the city's Yankee traders and moneylenders announced plans for an old fashioned fiesta, the reformers scurried down to

*A generation later, billboards on Wilshire Boulevard were defended by Foster & Kleiser as "a necessary force in stimulating and holding together the economy of the country."

City Hall to plump for an ordinance forbidding the wearing of masks "on the streets from sunset until sunrise during La Fiesta."

The Committee on Public Morals managed to keep a straight face when it reported to the council on a summer day in 1897: "Whereas, the morals of the City of the Angels have reached as near perfection as may be expected, we therefore see no further use for this committee, and recommend that this committee be discharged and stricken from the list of standing committees of this council." The recommendation was adopted.

·IV·
The Dizzy Decade,
1920-1929

"*It is inevitable that Los Angeles should
offer rare and glowing opportunities for faddists
and mountebanks. . . .*"

Willard Huntington Wright, 1913

Willard Huntington Wright, who surfaced from a sickbed in the
1920's as the popular mystery writer, S. S. Van Dine, was gradu-
ated from Santa Monica High School, where he set a record for
the 100-yard dash, and from St. Vincent's College, where class-
mates later remembered him for his modish wardrobe and his dazzling performance on the diamond and the gridiron. He did some
graduate work at Harvard and in 1910 went to work for the *Los
Angeles Times* as its literary editor. Three years later, *Smart Set*
published his classic putdown of Los Angeles. It could have appeared in last month's *Esquire*.

The city had grown too rapidly, Wright felt. Its population had reached nearly half a million, but temperamentally it was still an overgrown village, with "memories of the milk can, the new-mown hay, the Chautauqua lecturers, the plush albums, the hamlet devotions and the weekly baths." The new breed of Angeleno had come from the Middle West with "a complete stock of rural beliefs, pieties, superstitions and habits," along with "a righteous abhorrence of shapely legs" and "an aversion to late dinners, malt liquors, grand opera and hussies."

Wright gave the back of his hand to the city's restaurants ("little more than magnified village lunch rooms"), its lack of nighttime diversions ("the city's lights go out at twelve, and so does the drummer's hopes"), its cultural shortcomings ("at concerts they applaud the high notes"), its women ("they vote, storm the curbstone tables to sign petitions of protest") and its eccentrics ("spiritualists, mediums, astrologists, phrenologists, palmists, and all other breeds of esoteric windjammers").

Not surprisingly, when federal Prohibition descended on the land, January 16, 1920, no city in the country boasted a larger membership in the Women's Christian Temperance Union than Los Angeles. The ladies gathered for a day of "praise and prayer," while Al Levy draped his popular Spring Street watering hole in black crepe paper. His customers had anticipated the long dry spell ahead of them by laying away their share of the estimated $1,000,000 worth of illegal booze stashed inside the city.

Wright, like his friend Henry Mencken, had always been more at home in the fleshpots of San Francisco than in the uplifting lecture halls of Los Angeles, but when he traveled north in the early days of the Great Drought, he discovered with dismay that, even before passage of the Volstead Act, the state's temperance forces had managed to break the spirit of the Paris of the West. The bubbles had gone from its wine.

"No mere virtuous city like Los Angeles, whose piety is indigenous, could ever be so positively respectable," he reported, and went on to speculate that the difference between the morality of the two cities was "the difference between the virtue of a good man, instinctively generous and upright as a result of early training and environment, and the virtue of a reformed souse, who yesterday was moored to the brass rail, but who today is playing sour notes on a cornet in a Salvation Army band."

Casting about for some naughty, red-plush remnant of San Francisco's past, Wright stopped by a cafe once noted for its wickedness and fell into conversation with two dispirited women who might have been mistaken for "a brace of lady embalmers." He left the city saddened by its transformation. "There is something aggressively, inexorably decent and pseudo-elegant about a fallen lady under the pressure of propriety." he wrote, and added a bit of good news for Angelenos. For the first time in California history "the sojourner from Los Angeles is treated with consideration and respect in San Francisco."

✳ ✳ ✳

Two generations of East Coast journalists have paid their children's orthodontic bills by improvising variations on the themes Wright first sounded in *Smart Set* ("You can drink in a drive-in saloon, eat in a cafe shaped like a toad, and when you die, they will bury you in a 'Happy Cemetery,' " chortled the *Saturday Evening Post* in 1945), but few of them seem to have read his final paragraphs.

"The city reeks with promise." he declared, after speaking of the great problems being worked out within its borders. No city was more heterogeneous, he added and proceeded to praise its wit ("not the wit of epigram and culture, but the wit of serious endeavor"). He concluded with a vision of "a metropolis wealthy and diverse, commercially powerful and artistically wise."

Writing in the same year, 1913, Harris Newmark wound up his delightful and indispensable memoirs, *Sixty Years in Southern California*, with a forecast of the not distant day when the city he had first known as a dusty, adobe village diverting its sewage to the wilds of Sixth and Main would be "a world-center prominent in almost every field of human endeavor."

While Wright, the sophisticated critic, and Newmark, the pioneer merchant, were taking different routes across the city's lively past to reach the same conclusion about its future, crystal-ball gazers were looking ahead twenty-five years and giving *Times* readers a glimpse of the city as it might appear in 1938, when

Los Angeles High School (upper right) rises above a panoramic portrait of the city's commercial and industrial activity.

Angelenos would be nipping about in aermobiles and living in handsome apartments on Figueroa near Adams Boulevard, a district "sometimes compared to Riverside Drive in New York City."

In the up-to-date homes of 1938, automatic scrubbing machines, and electric vacuum cleaners would have "taken much of the manual work out of the hands of maids and oriental help," and each house would have its own refrigerating plant. Thanks to a new thermostat method of ventilation, it would not be necessary "to open a single window throughout the entire year, while still keeping the house freshened with the finest possible air and at a temperature desired."

"All the world joined in the craze to come to Los Angeles and secure a home in some of its environing valleys and mountains," the prophets declared, and projected a population of 1,532,000 by 1930.[*]

✳   ✳   ✳

Now that it was assured of sufficient water from the Owens Valley to meet the needs of 2,000,000 people, the *Times* had noted with satisfaction in 1905, Los Angeles found itself "in the novel position of exercising unusual power over industrial affairs and not simply over those within the city, but over even farming and horticulture and gardening operations from the head of the San Fernando Valley to the sea."

The city, in short, had its hand on the faucets of neighboring communities. If they wanted to drink, bathe and water their orange trees, they would have to submit to annexation by the City of Los Angeles. On New Year's Day, 1900, the city's area was 43 square miles. In the fall of 1923, when Ben Macomber of the *San Francisco Chronicle* looked in on the City Planning Commission, he learned that as of that particular day (October 6) the city limits encompassed 391.61 square miles.

"The map of Los Angeles is never completed," Macomber wrote, and found the city "intoxicated with its growth," but "the wise are reinforcing their optimism with caution."

Growth, like oil-drilling and movie-making, was a major local industry. More people meant more homes and apartments, and,

[*]It was 1,238,048 in 1930 and 1,504,277 in 1940.

64

thus, more customers for merchants, more deals for land speculators, more mortgages for moneylenders and more jobs for construction workers. When the real estate market collapsed in 1914, from 10,000 to 15,000 skilled mechanics left Los Angeles to find work in arms factories back east, and the city went through what a local financier later recalled as "six solid years of hell."

In 1920, however, while the rest of the country was suffering from a deflationary hangover, Los Angeles began to perk up. Out-of-work munitions workers headed west with their families, along with drifters and adventurers who had managed to scrape up the downpayment on a flivver, small farmers who had been starved out by falling prices and county seat lawyers and preachers who looked forward to spending their retirement years sprawled in the sun sucking oranges.

"Day after day, the whole week through, month by month, the great stream of humanity is flowing in," the Chamber of Commerce told a *Saturday Evening Post* writer. "There is no end to it. They are coming by train, by boat, by motor vehicle—any way to get here—one ceaseless pilgrimage. From all parts of the world they are coming. No human agency can stop them."

"We'd naturally like it much better if they would mail their money to us instead of coming themselves," remarked a longtime resident who had made a bundle on earlier waves of settlers and would undoubtedly profit from the new migration.

Downtown movers and shakers broke open their best bottles of pre-Volstead liquor on June 10, 1920 to toast the census tabulation which put Los Angeles ahead of San Francisco in population (575,480 to 508,410). "We deserve the honor," crowed a Chamber of Commerce official. Five Angelenos had sprung up where, twenty years earlier, there had been only one, but a businessman boasted that "the real growth of the town has just begun."

"Were you to soar above Los Angeles today in an airplane," *Leslie's* reported, "you would view a city that in area is the largest in the United States. You would see its outstanding features as, first of all, a huge gridiron of wide business and residence streets where thousands of motor cars skim about like great water spiders."

Years later, on a spring day in 1973, when John Pastier, the *Times* architecture critic, climbed into the passenger compartment of the Goodyear blimp and looked down on the city, he found it difficult to believe that "man could urbanize so much land in just a few decades." Except for its inadequate parks and for hillsides that developers had found too costly to mutilate, the only green spaces to be seen were cemeteries and golf courses. The rest of the land had been given over to homes and cars.

"Streets, freeways, parking areas and gas stations occupy perhaps as much space as residences," Pastier noted, "and this automotive domain is rarely pleasant from either the air or the ground."

* * *

"The traffic question has become a problem," the *Times* observed on December 18, 1910, and called on the City Council to do something "to keep the automobiles moving." Ten years later, when Rob Wagner was predicting that undertakers would soon be setting up branch mortuaries at all crossings and wags were referring to Los Angeles as "the city of the quick and the dead," the city fathers came up with a plan to protect pedestrians by outlawing parking in the downtown area.

"The problem before the City Council of making the downtown streets safe for democracy has stirred up a war that makes the Battle of Gettysburg seem like a checker game by comparison," the *Times* observed on January 3, 1920 when the ordinance was being debated.

It took effect the following April, and Angelenos awakened to the realization that, like it or not, they had become dependent on automobiles. A *Times* headline trumpeted the discovery: BUSINESS CAN'T DO WITHOUT THEM. Hollywood came to the rescue of downtown businessmen in the shapely form of Clara Kimball Young, who led a protest parade of cars through the business district. The no-parking ordinance was lifted, except for two evening rush hours. The city had capitulated to the automobile.

"Too bad we cannot make Broadway a three-deck affair," the *Times* sighed, momentarily struck by a fantasy which turned the streets over to automobiles, put public transportation underground

66

Broadway, looking northeast, on a quiet day in the early part of the Twentieth Century.

Stop-and-go signals make a brave stab at controlling Spring Street traffic.

and had pedestrians walking "on a viaduct level with the second floor of the shops." Fifty years later, dreaming of the Central City of 1990, city planners proposed what they call "pedways" to accomplish the same visionary objective.

"If we are a nation of extremes, Los Angeles is an extreme among us," Sarah Comstock informed readers of *Harper's* (May, 1928). She enjoyed the climate and the carnival atmosphere of the city, admired its new public library, delighted in the Hollywood Bowl's "Symphonies Under the Stars" and, after taking note of this "hurly-burly of speed, noise, light," came to the conclusion that "what Los Angeles is to excess, all our cities are to some extent."

"It suits me beautifully," Louis Adamic declared in a Haldeman-Julius Little Blue Book, *The Truth About Los Angeles* (1927), but in dealing with a city where Christianity ranked as a leading industry (just behind real estate and motion pictures), the author couldn't help being dismayed by a church advertisement listing the topics of a local pastor's next four Sunday sermons:

1. What Would Jesus Do If He Controlled the Street Railways of Los Angeles?
2. If He Were A Member of the Los Angeles City Council?
3. If He Were Owner of a Los Angeles Newspaper?
4. If He Were District Attorney of Los Angeles County?

* * *

In the early 1920's Angelenos worried about a possible power shortage, grumbled at having some 7,000 schoolchildren on half-day classes, adopted a zoning ordinance, took a spin along a newly opened stretch of Mulholland Drive ("destined to rank with the world's most magnificent drives") and, on New Year's Day, 1923, turned up for the dedication of the Angelus Temple. "I have never been so happy," beamed Sister Aimee Semple McPherson. She had arrived in Los Angeles, she recalled, with $10.

"My daughter, Myrabel, until a year ago, was attending a private school where the biblical explanation of creation was taught," a *Times* reader wrote the editor. "She was then a righteous and Christian maiden who had the highest ideals. She never smoked or swore.

"Then I sent Myrabel to one of our so-called 'Christian colleges' where she was compelled to study biology and its attending theory of evolution. I should have known better than to send her to these iniquitous colleges. After Myrabel had been taught evolution she no longer had the ideals that were hers before. Her self-respect is shattered. She has bobbed her hair; she uses cosmetics; she smokes and swears. Yesterday she fell so completely into the hands of the devil as to take liquor. I felt compelled to refuse her further admission into our home."

Not only were John Held, Jr. flappers bobbing their hair, painting their faces, smoking, swearing and drinking, they were also turning up their powdered noses at big, old fashioned church weddings. "It is considered much smarter now to be married in a casual, unobtrusive way," a syndicated columnist reported in 1922, and trotted out the testimony of sociologists to confirm what everybody already knew. Parental authority had suffered a mortal setback.

"Similarly," the columnist continued, "the husband's authority over his wife has greatly diminished . . . A wife is no longer her husband's absolute property as she was her father's before him . . . While in a few States in this country, women still have much the same legal status as they had under the patriarchal regime—which is to say, the status of slaves—throughout the greater part of the United States they are free and equal citizens."

Maiden ladies who, as teenagers, had wondered why an earlier generation had bundled Oscar Wilde off to jail were trying to figure out from newspaper accounts just what Fatty Arbuckle had done to that poor girl in San Francisco ("In the light of his record we find ourselves under the moral necessity of denying him the right to be a public entertainer," the Southwest Chamber of Commerce declared, and called on the Mayor and City Council to prohibit exhibition of his films.)

God-fearing Angelenos might shudder at the antics of the film colony, but the industry not only represented a weekly pay roll in 1924 of $1,500,000, it also drew tourists from all over the world. They drove out to the Fox studio at Sunset and Western, their autograph books at the ready in case Tom Mix came by, and window-shopped on Hollywood Boulevard, where, they had been told, "movie stars mingle with housewives and society matrons, so decorously garbed that they pass unnoticed on the streets."

Pilgrims found their way to Barbara La Marr's white mansion in Whitley Heights, Jack Holt's cream-colored English lodge in Laurel Cañon, William S. Hart's Sunset Boulevard spread and the nearby estate of Nazimova which later, as the celebrated Garden of Allah, would shelter Robert Benchley and Scott Fitzgerald, among others. Once they reached the Beverly Hills Hotel on their tour of the movie stars' homes, visitors took the advice of a fan writer and turned up "a hill road which leads through iron gates to 'Pickfair,' where dwell filmdom's gracious queen and her athletic husband."

Harry Carr, the *Times* columnist who had known the city since 1887, had watched it grow from 25,000 to 1,000,000. He had seen the handsome residences on Broadway turn into boarding houses and then give way to department stores. He remembered the Baker Block on Main Street near the Plaza when it had been a warren of law offices. Later the block had spawned the city's first fashionable apartments. When their day ended, the rooms had been taken over by penniless writers and artists who, Carr recalled, "gave studio parties and contested as to which could wear the funniest looking hair and talk the loudest."

Carr's memories included not only horse-drawn street cars, but also the city's first yacht-owners and the first two men reputed to be millionaires. "One was John Bradbury, who lived up on Court Street in the first fine house built here. The other was T. D. Stimson, who lived out in Figueroa Street. When we escorted visitors through the town, we showed them these two houses and we said to them with awe: 'He's got $1,000,000.' I don't think any of us really believed it. It was too prodigious. But it was part of looking over the town."

Easterners gaped at signs on recycled bungalows: HOME OF TRUTH and SOCIAL WIDOWHOOD CLUB, laughed at pulpit pronouncements ("If Jesus Christ was on earth today, He would be a Shriner") and went home with snapshots of the Children of the Sun Church, Pre-Astral Fraternity of Love and Nature-Way Medical College for Drugless Healing.

"I leave it to the sociologists to say whether cranks go to Cali-

The fruitful floor of the San Fernando Valley before developers took it in hand.

fornia, or Californians become cranks; whatever the process, results are wonderful," Bruce Bliven wrote the *The New Republic* (July 13, 1927) and wondered if someday a "real civilization" might not spring up in this rich, beautiful basin where "today not many civilized persons choose to live."

✳ ✳ ✳

In the 1920's, as in the 1880's, newcomers were welcomed to the city by land hustlers. Their buses lay in wait for prospects strolling the north end of Pershing Square. Once aboard, as the late W. W. Robinson recalled with relish, they formed a captive audience for spielers who pointed out such local landmarks as No. 56 Fremont Place (where Mary Pickford lived before she married Douglas Fairbanks), the Hollywoodland sign (Mack Sennett was building a million-dollar home on the hill above it) and the Talmadge Apartments (a million-dollar birthday gift to Norma Talmadge from her husband, Joseph W. Schenck).

Inevitably, of course, the spiel bore down heavily on the skyrocketing price of land in Los Angeles. In 1921 memberships in the Wilshire Country Club had gone begging at $100 each. A few years later, because of the increased value of the club's acreage, memberships were worth $5,000. Paramount Studios had bought two blocks in the Sunset and Vine area for $250,000. One was sold in the Twenties for $6,000,000.

"Don't Wait!" Janss Investment Company warned in 1923, when it offered lots in Westwood for as low as $950. "A few years ago," the copywriter pointed out, "lots between Western Ave. and Windsor Square—the heart of the high-priced Wilshire District—sold at similar low prices to those of Westwood today. Now they are worth as many thousands as they were hundreds." Prudent investors were advised to "buy on the high lands—away from fog, damp and mists."

By the end of 1924, the boom was petering out, but the *Times*, on New Year's day, 1925, was cheerfully certain that "the actual development of Los Angeles had just begun." To illustrate the dizzying rise of downtown real estate values, the paper traced the history of two lots in a tract the city had given Ozro W. Childs in 1864 for $1 and a promise to dig a zanja (ditch) to provide water for the vineyards and orchards in the southern part of town. Childs took title to some thirty city blocks bounded on the north and South by Sixth and Twelfth Streets, and on the east and west by Main and Figueroa.

Ten years later, two lots on the northwest corner of Eighth and Spring Streets, representing only a small fragment of the whole, were sold for $5,000. Twenty years went by and in 1894 they brought $30,000. By 1924 their estimated value was $1,650,000. The owner had picked them up a few years before for $375,000. Thus, in half a century the two lots had appreciated 164,900 per cent, the *Times* pointed out.

At 4 o'clock on the afternoon of July 15, 1926, the city's book borrowers got their first look at the new public library on Normal Hill.

"Without question one of the noblest buildings in America," tourists were told. "It follows no accented order of architecture, but through it strains of the Spanish, of the East, of the modern European, come and go like folk songs in a great symphony, rising to new and undreamed-of heights in an order truly American in spirit."

Oldtimers took a last nostalgic look at Temple Block ("warped and cracked with years") when it was razed in 1926 to clear space for a new City Hall. The City Council met in its new marble-pillared chamber for the first time on Monday, April 16, 1928. The building ("one of the most distinctive in the world") was formally opened ten days later and councilmen's friends went home clutching a souvenir volume.

"There is no particular style of architecture about the new municipal home," the text stated; "it is modern American. . . ."

✳ ✳ ✳

As the decade ended, downtown merchants were following their customers in the city's westward movement. In September, 1929, Bullock's opened its Wilshire branch "in recognition of the growing needs of a great city" and Silverwood's moved to the Miracle Mile, just across the street from Desmond's. In a single generation, Silverwood's had drifted south on Spring Street from the 100 to the 200 block, and then over to Sixth and Broadway before settling down on the recently reclaimed grain fields of Wilshire Boulevard.

"Westward the star of business takes its way," sang the *Times*.

All the while, however, the downtown skyline continued to be dominated by height-limit buildings. Twenty-three went up in 1926, twenty the following year. The Richfield Building, completed in 1929, was described as "an expression of modern art and thought." The architects (Morgan, Walls and Clements) had not only air-conditioned the entire building, but had arranged for its five passenger elevators to whisk motorists from the garage level to their offices. Bullock's-Wilshire, giving the automobile the same deference, had provided for a popular new service feature, off-street parking.

In late October, 1929, some 500 brokers, bankers and local functionaries assembled at 618 South Spring Street to watch a giant steam shovel, acting on a signal from the Mayor, break ground for the new $1,500,000 Los Angeles Stock Exchange. A week later the market collapsed.

◦ V ◦

Depression and "A Dream of Empire," 1930-1939

*"Señorita Los Angeles yesterday morning
threw wide the doors to her one
hundred and fiftieth birthday party with
colorful ceremonies upon the wide steps of
City Hall."*

Los Angeles Times, September 5, 1931.

The city's cuffs might be frayed and its bank account over-drawn, but to Mayor John C. Porter, a pious, Iowa-born dealer in used cars who had declared war on Communists and bootleggers, the Depression was merely a temporary deviation from a divine master plan for the metropolitan area.

"The situation is not at all alarming," he insisted. "We do not find it necessary to feed our unemployed men here. In San Francisco I saw free soup kitchens. There are none here."

In Los Angeles, as Duncan Aikman explained to readers of *The Nation*, "official confession of community distress is regarded as a heresy to the cult of boosterism." Thus, the feeding of down-and-out Angelenos was turned over to missions in the slum sections. A veteran missionary, chosen "the most useful citizen of Los Angeles," received a medal from the city fathers, only to have the muckraking *Los Angeles Record* sniff out the disclosure that he was serving decayed restaurant garbage. The mission asked the restaurants to provide more palatable scraps and the city's most useful citizen kept his medal.

"Why don't they take all that money and give employment with it or feed the poor?" malcontents grumbled when the city drew up plans for a ten-day fiesta to mark the one hundred and fiftieth anniversary of its founding.

As usual, the *Times* was standing by with an answer. The birthday party would "spread the fame of Los Angeles far and wide and bring in a harvest of tourists." Also, "this backward look through history, emphasizing as it does the difficulties which Los Angeles has overcome in becoming the city of today, puts present difficulties in perspective." The fiesta would help lift the city out of the commercial doldrums by lifting its spirits. As everyone knew, "much of the Depression is psychological."

✳ ✳ ✳

The blonde granddaughter of a Yankee banker reigned as queen of the fiesta. Mayor Porter got himself up as a ranchero and Governor James (Sunny Jim) Rolph, Jr., resplendent in black and gold, with a bright sash around his paunch, appeared to a *Times* reporter as "the true pioneer leader." Douglas Fairbanks, riding at the head of the motion picture contingent, "looked every inch a caballero." General Andres Pico was portrayed by a man named Murphy and Leo Carrillo played Leo Carrillo, the city's ceremonial Latino.

"This city has no money to waste on senseless decorations, flags, rodeos and other schoolboy stunts," Loren Miller complained in the local black paper, the *California Eagle*. "We are facing a winter in which hundreds of poor and destitute men, women and children will go without adequate food, clothing, and shelter."

Some 10,000 spectators, uncomfortable in the hot, late summer sun, jammed the Plaza for a reenactment of the myth-makers' conception of the pueblo's founding. Four acolytes in white surplices and red cassocks, carrying a cross and candles, led a procession of soldiers, priests and settlers. Eleven white couples, with twenty-two white children in tow, represented the forty-four black and brown *pobladores* who had come north from Mexico to establish the settlement on the banks of the Porciúncula.

A choir of forty male and female voices brought a lump to the throat of the *Times*. "If the spirits of those first inhabitants of El Pueblo were near, the strains of *When at Thine Altar*, a chant ascribed to the Cathedral of Cologne in 1623, must have sounded pleasingly familiar to their ears." More likely, the spirits of the settlers would have been wondering what had happened to their complexions.

"Those who saw the parade, and we have been assured that few Negroes did," the *California Eagle* declared, "must have a sense of the utter childishness of a race so saturated with prejudice that it attempts to change the color of its founders' skins. . . ."

At 1:35 A.M. on the pueblo's birthday, Major James H. Doolittle left Burbank and touched down at Newark, New Jersey, eleven hours and fifteen minutes later, setting a new transcontinental plane record. Next day, crossing the continent in the opposite direction on the Chief, Rudy Vallee's bride arrived in Los Angeles and was asked about life with the celebrated radio crooner. "Just an ordinary man," she replied.

Aviation and romance melded again at the close of the fiesta. Six planes of the California National Guard dropped high explosives on a mock-village near the airport, only to be upstaged by Sister Aimee Semple McPherson. Attractively turned out in one of "the new Eugenie hats and a modish blue suit trimmed with blue fox fur," she slipped off to Yuma, Arizona, in a chartered tri-motor plane and returned to Angelus Temple as the bride of a chubby young choir singer.

"God has rolled away my lonesomeness," purred Mrs. David L. Hutton.

Bride, bridegroom and mother-in-law, Mrs. Minnie (Ma) Kennedy ("My darling deserves the best in life") took up four col-

79

umns of the *Times*, leaving only one for the National Guard's preview of the destructive force of military aircraft. The pilots were hailed as "symbolic of all that is modern."

* * *

During the fiesta, someone rooting through the archives at the Title Guarantee and Trust Company dug up a letter written to the City Council by Major Henry Hancock* on a summer day in 1854. The pueblo's population at that time had been less than 1,600, but to the Mexican War veteran, a surveyor by profession, the shape of its future could already be determined.

"Los Angeles is no longer the quiet, peaceful and happy abode of Rancheros alone—its slumber is over—an impetus has been given her, she has assumed another character, is becoming a commercial mart, a nucleus around which are rallying all of the concomitant enterprises of a prosperous and flourishing inland city."

Speaking as "a surveyor of the innumerable and inviting valleys which surround you," Major Hancock urged city councilmen to stop disposing of city lots indiscriminately and to give some thought to securing common property "for the comfort and undivided enjoyment of the community at large." The letter turned up at a time when Angelenos were pleading for parks and public beaches, while the city continued to spread out in whatever direction land speculators found profitable to take it.

During the last decade the city had been engulfed in a human tidal wave. In 1920, with a population of 576,677, Los Angeles had ranked as the country's tenth largest city. Ten years later, with a population of 1,238,048, it was fifth. Looking back fifty years to a period when the city had been "the stepchild of the Pacific Coast," huddled on a desert, "scantily supplied with water and power, out of the track of progress," the *Times* attributed this prodigious growth to a single factor, the city's faithful adherence to "the American Plan or open-shop principle of industrial relations."

Only by waging a relentless fight against "the militant agres-

*Hancock Park is named for his son, who gave the Pleistocene animal trap to the county in 1915.

Downtown shoppers, on an agreeable pre-smog day when Men of Steel *was playing at Loew's State.*

Angels Flight, one of the city's favorite landmarks, now gone.

sions of unionism" had this inland seaport managed to surpass San Francisco, the editors claimed. Forty years earlier, the manufactured products of San Francisco had been thirteen times as valuable as those of Los Angeles. By 1927 the Southern California stepchild had forged ahead by a three-to-two margin. Any backsliding from the open-shop gospel, the *Times* warned, would cause the city's growth to "slow down, stop or even reverse its direction."

Los Angeles, in one generation, had shot up from a small town to a city to a metropolitan community, but its new urban dimensions had brought back the pueblo's ancient fear of a water famine. At the time city fathers first hit on the idea of tapping the Owens River, the local water supply had been about 72,000 acrefeet a year. By 1931 it was approximately 280,000 acre-feet, and history was repeating itself. Again the area's population had caught up with its available water resources.

"The growth experienced during the last quarter of a century cannot be duplicated in the same length of time—or ever, for that matter—if additional water is not obtained," the *Times* pointed out during the city's anniversary fiesta, when voters were mulling over a proposed $220,000,000 bond issue to bring water from the Colorado River to the cities in the metropolitan area.

The project was even more ambitious than Mulholland's Owens Valley aqueduct. Water was to be carried two hundred and forty-two miles from a lake below Hoover Dam to a reservoir from which it would have to be channeled another one hundred and fifty miles to the borders of the cities in the Metropolitan Water District. Work began in the depths of the Depression, when the first President from California (he had, of course, been born in Iowa) was preparing to turn the White House over to the Democratic Governor of New York, who had promised to cut down on government spending.

While downtown businessmen were plumping for passage of the Metropolitan Water District bonds, a conservative lawyer-banker, Jackson A. Graves, noticed a curious deterioration in the city's "matchless climate." On week-day mornings, when he left his home in Alhambra, the air was "fresh, pure, clean and invigorating," but when he got to the Central City, his vision was "impaired by dust, smoke, and the infinitesimal, invisible excrescences which arise from the crowded and much traveled streets and sidewalks. To me, the breathing of this atmosphere is extremely disagreeable; it gives me congestion of the head and nasal passages."

✳ ✳ ✳

Statistically, in this city of immigrants, every other Angeleno pinching the beefsteak tomatoes at the new Farmer's Market had been living somewhere else less than five years earlier. In the crowds outside Grauman's Chinese Theater, hoping to catch a glimpse of Clara Bow or Nancy Carroll at the premiere of a new talking picture, only a few old duffers could remember when Hollywood was a bone-dry rural community where retired shopkeepers sat in the shade of pepper trees wondering what the folks back home in Kansas were up to.

Some of the new Angelenos managed to live comfortably on the return from income property, others had struck it rich in oil or real estate. By their religious fervor in converting a tolerant, loose-living pueblo into a respectable, palm-shaded replica of their hometowns, all had contributed to Southern California's celebrated incongruities.

"The man with the hoe," Lillian Symes wrote in *Harper's* (June, 1931), "the horse trader, the crossroads storekeeper, the small-town evangelist may have dignity and fitness in his native setting. But dwelling in pseudo-tropical bungalows equipped with every modern gadget, playing horseshoes in shirtsleeves and suspenders beside a dazzling sea, disporting himself at Home State picnics under the eucalypti, inveighing against tobacco and the sins of the flesh in the shadow of the eternal mountains, he becomes slightly grotesque."

A new race of godlike creatures ("the men are bronze Apollos, the girls are golden Venuses") had been spawned by the "toil-worn, penny-saving peasants who, on a windy Kansas prairie, heard of the Garden of Eden and came west to invest in its real estate." While the old folks shambled off to Angelus Temple to hear Sister Aimee or to Trinity Methodist Church, where the Reverend Bob Shuler thundered against saloonkeepers, pornographers, white-slavers, political connivers and his sexy Echo Park

84

rival, young native Angelenos, born to sun and surf, headed for the beaches and the tennis courts.

It came as no surprise to Ms Symes that California athletes were conquering the world. "They are bigger, better and handsomer," she wrote, quite undone by "so much perfection in hair, teeth, skin and line." At times, after ogling young Ronald Colmans and Joan Crawfords darting down high school steps and playing miniature golf, she felt as though she had entered a "private playground set aside by the Hollywood studios for the picked choruses of the current musical talkies."

Twenty years had passed since the invasion of Hollywood by movie-makers. They had stumbled into the peaceful community of Christian teetotalers like a party of drunken convention delegates mistaking a vesper service for a stag film showing. By 1930, when the making of motion pictures had become as important to the local economy as drilling for oil and turning chaparral-covered hillsides into tract homes, most of the actors and the studios had moved away, but for tourists, it was enough to walk the same paved streets where their silent screen deities had disported themselves before they were taken off to Beverly Hills or Forest Lawn.

Mildred Adams, sketching the pueblo's portrait for the *New York Times* in the summer of 1930, was struck by the cultural clash of white Anglo-Saxon Protestant Hollywood and the Plaza, where Mexicans lived cheek-by-jowl with Chinese, Japanese, blacks and indigent whites in "a dark, crowded section, hot and thick, as full of mysterious ingredients as chili con carne, and as quick to burn." The Plaza was "a hotbed of vivid, violent life, as fertile as Hollywood is sterile."

Hollywood, for Robert Benchley, was "the dullest and most conventional community of its size in the country." Among its other deficiencies was an absence of speakeasies, "as the refined elements in other communities know speakeasies." The Plaza, for Aldous Huxley, was a fascinating "slum of Africans and Filipinos, Japanese and Mexicans. And what permutations and combinations of black, yellow and brown! What complex bastardies! And the girls—how beautiful in their artificial silk!"

Congestion and pollution come to the Olympic Boulevard conjunction of Spring and Main Streets in the 1950's.

On December 4, 1931, just three months after the pueblo kicked off its birthday celebration, the *Times* took note of its fiftieth anniversary by publishing a two-part supplement. One harked back fifty years to the day when "there appeared on the doorsteps of a sleepy, little frontier town on the edge of the desert, a few hundred copies of a four-page newspaper," and the other described the world of 1981, as viewed by such distinguished contributors as:

Lee De Forest: "Television sets will be in every modern home."

Douglas Fairbanks: "When you get into the theater of the future, it will be just as though you were sitting in this room as I am now. The screen will be big enough for your eye to rove about on it and come back to the main action."

Sir Oliver Lodge: "We will be communicating with our departed dead."

The Very Reverend William R. Inge, Dean of St. Paul's, London: "The rational costume for both sexes—cheap, becoming and scanty —will enable beauty to be recognized in the body and limbs as well as in the face."

Owen Johnson, writing on the liberated woman: "She will lay down the terms on which she will reproduce the race."

Dr. R. A. Millikan: "When coal and oil are gone, science will find a way to utilize the energy of the sun.

Sir James Jeans: "It may be that science will in time discover how to transform atomic energy into power. If this vision is realized, even partially, the curse which fell on Adam will be lifted, and heavy manual labor will almost disappear from life."

Henry Ford: "Public charity will be an ancient dream and no longer a reality."

Albert Einstein: "Enlightened peoples will learn to abhor war and refuse to participate in it."

Eric Temple Bell: "By 1945 Prohibition will cease to be an issue. Substitutes for gin, with forty times the potency and no ill effects, will be on sale at soda fountains."

William B. Stout: "One can leave New York after breakfast and arrive in Los Angeles in time for evening dinner."

Learned men foresaw a brave new world of television and transcontinental flights, a world free of wars, welfare, hangovers and unwanted children, but, reviewing the predictions a generation later, nothing seems wider of the mark that Bryant Hall's prize-winning essay on life in Los Angeles in 1981.

The city fathers, in Hall's vision of the future, had done away with downtown parking, billboards, power poles and overhead wires. Public buildings in the new Administrative Center were tucked into what appeared to be "an enormous park or garden, traversed by broad, tree-lined avenues." Thanks to farsighted city and county planners, Angelenos roamed freely along beaches from Santa Monica to Laguna, "nearly all publicly owned."* Commuters and sightseers moved around the metropolitan area on "the finest system of urban and interurban transportation ever developed." No one ever had to wait more than thirty seconds for a bus.

Such was the dream in 1931. The reality was reported by a *New York Times* correspondent: "The city has no subways, its bus lines and its street car systems are hopelessly inadequate, if you want a taxicab you must telephone and then wait until a driver can be waked up and sent forth."

* * *

"It hit hard in Los Angeles," Matt Weinstock later wrote of the Depression. "The unemployment and relief rolls were in the tradition of the biggest and best; but during those bad years, while things were at half speed, people rediscovered the city. They couldn't afford night clubs, or the fancy places, so they went to the zoo and Griffith Park. They ducked Palm Springs and the High Sierras in favor of a picnic in Mint or Bouquet Canyon, or their back yards. The economic pressure taught them a great lesson: a person couldn't have his malnutrition in a nicer place than Los Angeles."

While the unemployed took the sun in Pershing Square and hungered for bread, the city fathers gave them a circus, the Tenth Olympiad. A million-dollar Coliseum designed to seat 75,000 spectators went up on state land in Exposition Park and, for an-

---

*"Southern California's greatest single resort asset—the public beaches—is slowly but surely diminishing in size," the *Times* warned on August 15, 1926 in a feature article headlined: COUNTY'S BEACH PLAYGROUNDS PASSING TO PRIVATE HANDS.

other million, its seating capacity was boosted to 105,000, making it the world's largest sports arena. Every seat was taken when the games opened on July 30, 1932, and when they closed on August 14, leaving only three previous Olympic records unbroken.

"This idea of the athletes of the world living together as neighbors will go a long way toward promoting world peace," said the secretary of the Netherlands Olympic Committee after visiting Olympic Village.

Japanese athletes were not swept off their feet by Los Angeles. The streets and buildings, they were surprised to find, were no more modern than those of Tokyo, and some were inferior. They were also dismayed by their hosts' casual dress. "Thousands thronged the city coatless and many without their neckties," they told the *Japan Times* when they returned home.

At the games, they reported, they had been treated fairly and courteously by officials and by spectators, but in the evening, when they had set out to dine in one of the city's better restaurants, they had been turned back at the door with the curt explanation, "Mexicans are not admitted." "We are not Mexicans, we are Japanese," they had explained, only to discover that this made matters worse.

"Most disgusting of all," continued the *Japan Times* story, "was the fact that the second generation Japanese and those resident in California took such a situation for granted. . . ."

✳ ✳ ✳

During the depressed decade of its sesquicentennial, Los Angeles annexed Tujunga (1932), set up a branch office of City Hall in Van Nuys to serve the San Fernando Valley (1933) and dedicated the Griffith Park Planetarium (1935). Long-suffering Angelenos, for the first time in the pueblo's history, recalled their mayor. Frank L. Shaw was replaced by, to quote *Time*, "pudgy, petulant Fletcher Bowron."

"I feel certain that I will prove to be an unpopular mayor," he said, and proceeded to keep getting himself reelected, giving rise to the political axiom, "No one seems to like him except the voters."

As the 1930's drew to a close, William Powell was teamed with Myrna Loy for another Thin Man film, Charlie McCarthy was chosen grand marshal of the 1940 Tournament of Roses parade (it was to be telecast for the first time, going into the homes of some seven hundred owners of television sets, thanks to the pioneers at W6XAO), and Los Angeles County was not only still the nation's leading agricultural county, but was also producing more than half of its airplanes.

Angelenos, in 1939, celebrated two historic achievements, completion of the Union Passenger Terminal and the main line of the Colorado River Aqueduct. A generation later, the railroad station would be empty, the Colorado River water supply inadequate, and local breadwinners would be lining up for unemployment benefits because the flow of money from Washington for space travel had slowed to a trickle.

Half a million Angelenos turned out on May 3, 1939 to have a look at the new railroad station across from the Plaza. It was the "most modern terminal in America," they were told, and in all the excitement over its formal opening, nobody bothered to check the industry's economic pulse. In the last ten years the railroads had laid off half of their employees and two-thirds of their total mileage was in serious difficulties or bankrupt.

Six months later, on November 19, cool, clear water from the Colorado River traveled two hundred and forty-two miles through tunnels, open canals, conduits and siphons from Lake Havasu to Riverside, where it would be stored until it was carried another one hundred and fifty miles to the other cities of the Metropolitan Water District.

"It is a dream of empire coming true before our eyes," said W. P. Whitsett, chairman of the district's board of directors.

With the aqueduct splashed across the front page, little attention was paid to a brief wire service story filed from Berkeley: "Dr. Ernest O. Lawrence, 38-year-old University of California professor who recently was awarded the Nobel Prize in physics, announced tonight he has been asked by the University of Texas to continue his atom-smashing experiments there."

WILL IT EVER END?

Reprinted from the Los Angeles Times, December 11, 1910.

· VI ·

War and Peace, 1940-1949

*"After four frantic years of war and
four wild years of peacetime boom, it is plain
that Los Angeles will never be like anything
else on earth."*

Time, July 4, 1949.

Matt Weinstock was on record against Sunday driving ("a form of madness"), but on Sunday, December 7, 1941, he drove his wife, Hilda, down to Puente, where friends had a walnut ranch. Not until the Weinstocks got home that afternoon did they hear about the bombing of Pearl Harbor.

"A neighbor told us as we got out of our car," Matt wrote in his *Daily News* column. "This is unimportant except that people may remember in years to come exactly what they were doing the day Japan attacked the U.S."

Kenji Nakauchi, Japan's slight, bespectacled young consul, with a son of high school age back home, learned of the air raid while out for a walk.

93

"I knew the situation was serious, but I didn't know it was this serious," he told reporters who came to his door at 7425 Franklin Avenue, and when pressed for a comment, he threw up his hands. "What can I say except that I am quite sorry?"

There were some 40,000 residents of Japanese ancestry in the Los Angeles area, he estimated, and they were about evenly divided between Issei (those born in Japan) and Nisei (those born in the United States). The consul saw no reason why either first or second generation Japanese should be taken into custody. He cited his experience in Vancouver, where he had been stationed at the time Canada went to war with Germany and Italy.

"All the Germans and Italians were not locked up," he said.

Little Tokyo was stunned, but its cafes, bars and newsstands stayed open. "We will obey the law," an elderly Issei remarked, and went on watering plants in front of his florist shop. A middle-aged neighbor found it hard to believe that the Japanese Government had ordered the attack. "Couldn't it be possible," he speculated, "that Germans might have, in some manner, got hold of Japanese planes and carried out the bombing?"

Harbor officials quarantined the Japanese fishing fleet and when the *S.S. Catalina* docked at Wilmington, an agent of the Federal Bureau of Investigation was on hand to scrutinize the sightseers. In its efforts to leave no subversive stone unturned, the FBI descended on the Zamorano Club, only to discover it was a goodly fellowship of politically conservative book collectors who had named their organization after California's first printer, Agustin Zamorano (1798-1842).

* * *

A yellow signal, indicating the approach of enemy aircraft went out over the state-wide police teletype at 7:55 P.M., Wednesday, December 10. Six minutes later, KFI, the city's key radio station in times of emergency, announced "a complete blackout immediately from Bakersfield to San Diego and as far east as Boulder City and Las Vegas." All other radio stations went off the air.

Shortly after eight o'clock Fire Department sirens sounded for one minute and street lights winked out. Air raid wardens traipsed through the darkened streets, warning housewives to douse the lights of their Christmas trees and drape blankets across their windows. Pedestrians fumbling their way home were bowled over by motorists driving without headlights. Every ambulance at the city's command was pressed into service.

All next day Angelenos were bombarded with radio warnings of a trial blackout set for 9 o'clock that night, but two hours before the city was to turn off its lights, the test was cancelled. Suddenly at 9:42, however, an Air Raid Warning Service yellow light flashed the message: "Raiding party on the way." After an hour's confusion as to whether they were being subjected to a test or a possible air attack, Angelenos heard the all-clear and tumbled back into bed, only to be awakened at 2:50 A.M. by another alarm. Local radio stations went off the air and the city waited for the enemy planes that never showed up. The all clear sounded at 4 o'clock.

Ordinarily police would have expected an average of twenty-five burglaries and five robberies during the period of the blackout. Instead there had been no burglaries and only three holdups. One person had been arrested, a recalcitrant drunk who had refused to extinguish the lights in his house.

$$* \quad * \quad *$$

The blackout that still sticks in the memories of middle-aged Angelenos, the mysterious battle of Los Angeles, took place in the early morning hours of February 25, 1942. The stage was set on February 23, when a Japanese submarine, I-17, surfaced near Santa Barbara and pumped thirteen rounds of 5½-inch shells into an oil installation at Ellwood.

Next evening, around 7 o'clock, the Navy received warning from Washington of an impending attack on Los Angeles. Five hours later the military's then-secret radar screens picked up an unidentified target about 120 miles west of the city. At 2:27 the object appeared to be only three miles away. At 3:06 something resembling a balloon was sighted over Santa Monica and antiaircraft batteries were ordered to open fire.

"The gunfire brought everyone to a window or front porch," Newsweek later recalled. "Golden tracers arched upward in the blackness. More than 1,400 three-inch shells were fired. Shrapnel whistled down to clatter on hard pavement or imbed itself in yards and houses. But no bombs were dropped."

The Army had been shooting at clouds, the Secretary of the Navy suggested, but the Secretary of the Army stood firm on his statement that unidentified planes had, indeed, appeared over the city. Although Lieutenant General John L. DeWitt, commanding general of the Western Defense Command, thought it "possible" that the aircraft had been launched from a Japanese submarine, he considered it "more likely" that they had been civilian planes operated by unauthorized pilots.

A spokesman for the Japanese Navy joined the debate in the fall of 1945. No Japanese planes had flown over Los Angeles during the war, he said, and only one had taken off from a submarine surfacing near the West Coast. It had circled above Southern Oregon on February 9, 1942, with orders "to attack military installations but the lone plane was unable to discover any."

On the twentieth anniversary of the battle, a *Times* reporter in Washington burrowed into the archives, hoping to clear up the mystery. Official records, he found, were so confused and contradictory ("and," a classified document added, "the subsequent testimony of eyewitnesses, both civilian and military, complicates rather than clarifies them") that it was impossible to reconstruct the story.

* * *

On the eve of their first wartime Christmas, Angelenos checked their supplies of candles and flashlight batteries, laid in an extra bag of sugar and stayed within reach of their radios. Bob Hope spent Christmas with his family. Robert Taylor and Barbara Stanwyck entertained the Jack Bennys in their new Beverly Hills home. Corporal Jimmy Stewart was at Moffett Field and Mickey Rooney was planning to marry an 18-year-old actress from North Carolina named Ava Gardner.

In the first seventy-two hours after the Pearl Harbor attack, FBI agents had rounded up three hundred and sixteen Japanese, seventy-three Germans and eleven Italians. By Christmas, when local jails bulged with suspected fifth columnists, their wives,

This day, too, will live in infamy.

A young Angeleno, April, 1942.

Courtesy California Historical Society

My own, my native land—July, 1945.

Anglo servicemen make war on Chicanos in the downtown area—
June, 1943.

A young Pachuco, *stripped of his "zoot suit," comforts a riot victim.*

parents and friends were pleading with United States immigration authorities for permission to visit the prisoners, many of whom were American citizens.

"They are being well fed and kept comfortable—and if found innocent of any connection with the enemy, they will be released," an immigration official explained to the press, and cheerfully added: "Meanwhile, we are showing them how democracy works."

✳   ✳   ✳

"A hell of a thing, especially for an American citizen," Tom Ikkanda, a service station owner on Olympic Boulevard, grumbled to himself when he first heard rumors that concentration camps were being prepared for Japanese-Americans.

On February 19 President Roosevelt issued Executive Order 9066, authorizing the designation of military areas "from which any or all persons may be excluded." Little Tokyo bristled with signs, CLOSING OUT SALE. Some offered discounts up to fifty percent on their belongings; others simply asked prospective buyers to make an offer.

The first contingent of Japanese Angelenos, aliens and citizens alike, left for the hastily built evacuees' city of Manzanar on March 21. American children wearing Superman tee-shirts and Shirley Temple frocks were carted off to the Owens Valley with their parents and grandparents. No wrongdoing had been charged or proved. Guilt no longer had to be established in a court of law according to prescribed procedures. Now it could be inherited.

"We're charged with wanting to get rid of the Japs for selfish reasons," a spokesman for Salinas Valley growers and shippers told a *Saturday Evening Post* stringer. "We might as well be honest. We do. It's a question of whether the white man lives on the Pacific Coast or the brown man."

✳   ✳   ✳

"Race does not lie in the language but exclusively in the blood," wrote Adolf Hitler, and, in the summer of 1942, his Berlin radio station was happy to quote similar sentiments expressed in a report prepared by the Los Angeles County sheriff's office, setting forth the official explanation of juvenile delinquency in the Mexican-American *barrios*.

"The Caucasian, especially the Anglo-Saxon, when engaged in fighting, particularly among youths, resort to fisticuffs and may at times kick each other, which is considered unsportive; but this Mexican element considers all that to be a sign of weakness, and all he knows and feels is a desire to use a knife or some lethal weapon. In other words, his desire is to kill, or at least let blood ... When there is added to *this inborn characteristic* that has come down through the ages, the use of liquor, then we certainly have crimes of violence." (Emphasis added.)

Violence, in short, was presumed to be in the liquor-heated blood of these brown-skinned youngsters whose forebears had founded the pueblo which now excluded them from so many public parks and pools, theaters, dance halls and restaurants, but not from selective service.

"We are Americans for the draft, but Mexicans for jobs and the police," young men complained.

This generation of Mexican-American Angelenos had sprung from the Depression years, when the city's Spanish-speaking shops and cafes were drifting away from the Plaza, inching south as far as Third and Fourth Streets, engulfing ten-cent stores and movie houses along the way.

"Being strangers to an urban environment," Carey McWilliams points out in *North From Mexico* (1948), "the first generation had tended to respect the boundaries of the Mexican communities. But the second generation was lured far beyond these boundaries into the downtown shopping districts, to the beaches, and above all, to the 'glamor' of Hollywood. It was this generation of Mexicans, the *pachuco* generation, that first came to the general notice and attention of the Anglo-American population."

The *pachuco* adopted as his uniform the "drape-shape" or, as it was called outside the *barrios*, the "zoot-suit." To the police, inflamed by the sight of the pleated, peg-topped, high-waisted trousers and the long, loose, wide-shouldered coats, the bizarre costume identified young gangsters who, from time to time, had to be rounded up and worked over.

In August, 1942, when the body of young José Díaz was found

in the vicinity of an abandoned gravel pit near Slauson and Atlantic Boulevards (a local newspaperman dubbed it "The Sleepy Lagoon"), police arrested twenty-four young Mexican-Americans, including two who had signed up with the United States Navy. On January 12, 1943, twelve of the defendants were found guilty of murder and five of assault.

The evidence against them was so flimsy that their convictions were overturned by the District Court of Appeal, but not before eight of the young men had served nearly two years in San Quentin. Corridors of the Hall of Justice swarmed with exultant families, friends and neighbors on the late October day in 1944 when the prisoners were set free.

"For the first time in the history of Los Angeles," wrote Carey McWilliams, who served as chairman of the Sleepy Lagoon Defense Committee, "Mexicans had won an organized victory in the courts and, on this day, bailiffs and deputy sheriffs and court attaches were looking rather embarrassed in the presence of Mexicans."

In the meantime, while the Sleepy Lagoon youngsters were still behind bars, trouble had broken out in Venice between *pachucos* in "drapes" and some teenage Anglos reinforced by sailors spoiling for a fight. "The only thing we could do to break it up," a police officer later recalled, "was to arrest the Mexican kids." Inflammatory reports in the local press ("guerilla gang warfare," "youthful terrorists," "juvenile hoodlums," "reign of terror") helped make an explosion inevitable.

It was sparked on the night of Thursday, June 3, 1943, after eleven sailors walking along the 1700 block of North Main Street were set upon by what they described as a gang of zoot-suiters. Next evening some two hundred sailors took over a fleet of taxicabs (how they found the cabs remains a mystery) and invaded the east side *barrios*, leaving four youths lying on blood-stained pavements. Nine sailers were arrested, but no charges were ever brought against them.

The Army and the Marine Corps joined the Navy in the following night's assault. Arms linked, the servicemen stormed the downtown streets four abreast. Civil and military authorities obligingly looked the other way, but when some young Mexican-Americans gathered on a street corner, they were promptly packed off to jail. On Sunday, June 6, sailors beat up eight *barrio* teenagers and wrecked a bar on Indiana Street. The police made forty-four arrests. All were Mexican-American and all had been badly mauled. The *Daily News* account was headlined:

44 ZOOTERS JAILED IN
ATTACKS ON SAILORS

On Monday night, a mob of several thousand servicemen and civilians swarmed over the Central City, halting street cars and breaking into theaters, dragging *pachucos* out into the streets, stripping them naked and beating them senseless. It was a Mexican version of the Chinese Massacre of 1871, and it lost little in the translation. Local authorities, then as earlier, not only made no serious effort to stop the bloodletting, some even joined in the evening's sport. Al Waxman, editor of *The Eastside Journal*, described an incident he witnessed at Twelfth and Central.

"Four boys came out of a pool hall. They were wearing zoot-suits that have become the symbol of a fighting flag. Police ordered them into arrest cars. One refused. He asked: 'Why am I being arrested?' The police officer answered with three swift blows of the night-stick across the boy's head and he went down. As he sprawled, he was kicked in the face. Police had difficulty loading his body into the vehicle because he was one-legged and wore a wooden limb. Maybe the officer didn't know he was attacking a cripple.

"At the next corner a Mexican mother cried out, 'Don't take my boy, he did nothing. He's only fifteen years old. Don't take him.' She was struck across the jaw with a night-stick and almost dropped the two and a half year old baby that was clinging in her arms. . . ."

"Most of the citizens of the city have been delighted with what has been going on," beamed the *Eagle Rock Advertiser*, echoing the pueblo's vigilante past, and County Supervisor Roger Jessup might well have been draped across the Bella Union bar in the 1850's knocking back a shot of rye whisky with Major Horace Bell when he delivered himself of the opinion, "All that is needed to end lawlessness is more of the same action. . . ."

* * *

Roger Butterfield snapped a candid portrait of Angelenos at war on an assignment for *Life* (November 22, 1943). "We get four crops from our Victory Gardens," he was told by a backyard farmer, who also delighted in being able to "go swimming any day in the year." Paddock Engineering Company had orders for more than 1,000 postwar pools and livewires at Forest Lawn were preparing a helicopter field "to receive funeral processions from the air."

"I never dreamed there was such a place," a North Dakota soldier had told one of Butterfield's informants. "I'm coming back here to live after the war."

The young civilian soldiers streaming through Union Passenger Terminal caught a glimpse of blue skies and palm trees, sniffed the exotic odors of Olvera Street, hitchhiked out to the Hollywood Canteen to dance with drama majors from Iowa and flew off to the South Pacific dreaming of a postwar life built around beach parties at Malibu and backyard barbecues in the Hollywood Hills.

While the GI's were writing V-mail letters from bomb-torn atolls, a European philosopher of history, Paul Schrecker, took a brief, horrified look at Los Angeles (somebody tried to sell him an "Idealistic Hamburger"). "The city seems not like a real city resulting from natural growth," he decided, "but like an agglomeration of many variegated movie sets, which stand alongside one another but have no connection with one another." Writing in *Harper's* (September, 1944) at a time when the word "smog" was just coming into common usage, he predicted that the boom town "might soon become the most populated place in the world—or a ghost town just as well."

Two years later, when Angelenos got the Christmas issue of *Newsweek*, they found most of one page taken up with a report on their smog. Nobody knew where to fix the blame ("dumps, lumberyard incinerators, locomotives, Diesel trucks, an asphalt plant, and oil refineries" were leading candidates), but everybody suffered from the acrid fumes and the city's boosters were squirming over a headline in the *St. Louis Globe-Democrat:*

BEAUTIFUL, SUNNY CALIFORNIA, EH?
LOS ANGELES NOW NO. 1 SMOG TOWN

✳ ✳ ✳

The war officially ended at 4 o'clock, Los Angeles time, Tuesday, August 14, 1945. The siren on top of the *Times* building screamed the news to downtown shoppers and office workers, touching off a monumental traffic jam. Servicemen kissed every girl in sight, including the plain ones, and many of the babies born that day were to go through life as Victor or Victoria. The Mayor intruded a sobering note on the carnival.

"Peace," he pointed out, "threatens industrial dislocation in this area which might throw thousands out of work."

Los Angeles, "the arsenal of democracy," was still the seat of the nation's richest agricultural county, but by the end of the decade, as *Time* reported in a cover story (July 4, 1949), its economy no longer rested on oil fields, citrus groves, film studios and aircraft plants.

"It lands more fish than Boston or Gloucester, makes more furniture than Grand Rapids, assembles more automobiles than any other city but Detroit, makes more tires than any other city but Akron. It is a garment center (bathing suits, slacks, sports togs) second only to New York. It makes steel in its backyard. Its port handles more tonnage than San Francisco."

In an earlier day, asthmatic druggists and dairymen had moved to Los Angeles to take the sun and pick oranges from their own trees. Now Rexall Drug and Carnation were moving their corporate headquarters to Los Angeles, joining the city's new generation of veterans and defense workers. It was impossible to build enough schools and hospitals, install enough telephones, provide enough sewers and parking lots. The overgrown pueblo had become a prisoner of its own technological wonder-working.

"The good Lord didn't intend this to be an industrial city," declared Mayor Bowron, adhering to the downtown tradition of linking the city's development with celestial planning.

Whatever providence may have intended for the Los Angeles basin, the City Hall observation deck on a clear day in 1949 commanded a view of thousands of acres of smoke stacks, assembly plants, warehouses, refineries and processing plants, interspersed with new factory towns sheltering the families of migrant

With the lifting of the city's height restrictions, skyscrapers re-make the Central City skyline in the 1970's.

workers who had come to the metropolitan area to find jobs in defense plants and had stayed on to plague city officials with their demands for schools, hospitals, libraries, parks and playgrounds.

"For the past fifteen years," Carey McWilliams wrote in *Harper's* (October, 1949), "the city has shown the incompetence of an idiot giant in dealing with its affairs. The story of this vast city's bungling of such problems as traffic, transportation, spoiling of its beaches, the sewage, smog, and related items would make a monumental municipal comedy of errors."

Westchester illustrated his point. In 1940 it had been open country, much of it planted in lima beans. By the end of the decade, some 30,000 people, most of them young, were living in West-chester. The city had no fire or police stations, no emergency hospital facilities, not even a barber shop. Its library was "about as big as a boxcar" and its elementary schools consisted of "hastily thrown together bungalows." Nothing had been planned. Like the child of a summer cruise romance, the city had just happened.

The prologue to the metropolitan area's postwar difficulties had been recited six weeks before the attack on Pearl Harbor, when city planners and architects took over seven galleries of the Los Angeles Museum of History, Science and Art for an exhibition contrasting what the metropolis had become and what it might be.

"A topographic panorama showed visitors what a beautiful place Los Angeles County had been before the Angelenos had got there," *Time* reported. "Other panoramas depicted the idyllic cattle and sheep ranches of a century or more ago, the land and oil booms of the 1880's and '90s, the leaning fences and signboards of the 1920s. The 1941 display pictured children playing in congested streets, oil wells blossoming on front lawns. A weather-beaten shack, transplanted whole from a Los Angeles slum, stood accusingly before a backdrop of Los Angeles' skyscraping city hall."

In the city planner's projection of their future, Angelenos lived in a spacious, sun-drenched world where homes and factories were separated by recreational greenbelts, where poverty had been swept from view and cars sped safely along one hundred miles of projected parkways (only fifteen miles of which had actually been built).

Less than a year earlier, on December 30, 1940, the West's first freeway, a six-mile stretch of "miracle boulevard," had been thrown open to the public. The Arroyo Seco Parkway* had made Pasadena a twelve-minute drive from downtown Los Angeles. Compton, as city planners liked to point out, was the same distance from the Central City—nine miles—but the trip took thirty-five minutes. In the 1941 exhibition, ". . . Now We Plan," the city's future was committed to the automobile and the freeway.

"I suppose we should not condemn those original planners so much because they could not foresee the adverse effects of the freeway," Larry E. Moss, the Sierra Club's Southern California representative, recently remarked to Al Martinez of the *Times*. "But we should chastise those who, in the 1950s and the 1960s, knew better and, knowing better, still continued to buy the cloudy vision."

✳ ✳ ✳

If one day in the life of the postwar metropolis could be brought back for dissection by some urban pathologist probing for the early warning symptoms of the city's present disorders, February 6, 1947 might serve as well as any other. It was a warm, winter day, when the smog was somewhat worse than usual. There was a slight earthquake some one hundred miles distant at 9:30 that morning and the nation's airlines were bruising their backs with self-congratulatory slaps at having come up with a noise abatement program. In Sacramento, oil and trucking lobbyists had managed to beat down Governor Earl Warren's highway improvement bill.

"Every month of delay will mean we will continue to have at least three hundred people killed and six thousand injured, many unnecessarily," the Governor snapped, and took off for Washington, where he was to testify on behalf of water development and flood control in the Central Valley.

The temperature in downtown Los Angeles had hit 80° the day before and a twelve-foot, cigar-shaped torpedo had fallen on Burbank from a military plane. A more generous sugar ration stamp, good for ten pounds, would soon be available. It reminded Matt

*Its name was changed to the Pasadena Freeway in 1954.

Weinstock's readers of the remote day in 1942 when Angelenos had gone to their neighborhood elementary schools to sign up for ration books and a Beverly Hills matron, asked how much sugar she had on hand, had replied, "Three lumps."

Police were running down another false lead in the Black Dahlia murder case. Mae West was making a personal appearance at the Biltmore Theater and *The Drunkard* was in its fourteenth year. Moviegoers could choose among *The Best Years of Our Lives*, *The Jolson Story* and *The Razor's Edge*. Catholic students had called a mass meeting in the hope of launching a month-long boycott of movie houses to protest the current wave of obscene films.

In its daily box recording the previous day's "smoke" conditions, the *Times* noted that visibility at the Civic Center had been cut from ten miles at 10 o'clock in the morning to two miles by midafternoon. "To a person who knew Los Angeles in her better days," said one of the doctors in town for a rheumatic fever conference, "this smog is most regrettable. It makes for more respiratory irritations—which in turn tend toward more respiratory diseases. These lead to more rheumatic fever."

"It's impossible," Evelyn Waugh grunted when reporters followed his spoor to the Bel-Air Hotel and asked for an audience. Betty Crocker was celebrating her silver anniversary with Gold Medal Flour and Sonny Wisecarver, having run off at the age of fourteen with a twenty-one-year-old housewife and two years later with another married woman, this one nine years his senior, had bobbed up in Las Vegas, where he hoped to find work and get married. The 18-year-old paramour had his eye on a girl of 16.

A generation after General Otis had gone to a non-union grave, Charles E. Wilson, president of General Motors, was telling a Senate committee that he would take up farming rather than submit to a union contract. The Dow Jones industrial average had hit 182.52, the highest level in five months. Eddie Arcaro had brought in two winners at Santa Anita and Babe Ruth, on the eve of his fifty-third birthday, was "feeling fine." Rear Admiral Richard E. Byrd was puttering about the South Pole and Margaret Truman had moved out of the White House and taken an apartment in New York.

While Republican Congressmen were trampling the grave of

Franklin D. Roosevelt by supporting a proposed constitutional amendment limiting Presidents of the United States to two terms, Representative Helen Gahagan Douglas ("the gentlewoman from California," as the Speaker called her) made the shocking statement that "more families are homeless in Los Angeles today than after the San Francisco earthquake or the Johnstown flood."

An estimated 162,000 families, including 50,000 veterans, were holed up in tents, garages, cabins, trailers and firetrap hotels. After reminding her colleagues that they had appropriated two billion dollars during the war years to run up cantonments, Mrs. Douglas pointedly asked, "Do you have to go to war to get a roof over your head?" Her eloquent plea on behalf of her Veterans' Emergency Housing Bill didn't make the *Times* next day, but space was found on the front page for a wire service story on a Florida cold wave.

*Bunker Hill looks out over the westward shift of the city's
financial heartland.*

·VII·
The Megalopolis, 1950-1969

---

*"Your city government is moving steadily
forward into a decade which is the most
promising in our history."*

Mayor Fletcher Bowron, 1950.

Los Angeles, in 1950, was well on its way to becoming the nation's
fourth largest city or, as some insisted, the world's largest parking lot. Its air was foul and its traffic congested, but the county's
air pollution watchdogs were confident that by summer they
would reach "the turning point in the war on smog" and the state's
freeway builders were counting on their superhighways to move
Angelenos about the basin at a merry clip.

By the time the decade ended, however, the air was more noxious than ever, the freeways were clogged and Mayor Bowron
had been swept from office by a colorless, *Times*-backed Congressman, Norris Poulson, who attacked the incumbent for his
failure to provide a mass rapid transit system, a charge his succes-
sor would be fielding twenty years later in an unsuccessful bid for
a fourth term.

Mayor Poulson is remembered not for a modern system of transportation but for the lopsided real estate deal that installed the Brooklyn Dodgers in Chavez Ravine. "We love our city and we weep for it," groaned the *Times* when Sam Yorty moved into City Hall in 1961. He, too, made no memorable progress in tidying up the city's air or its traffic. Instead, he integrated its rubbish.

"We cannot build enough expressways to handle traffic in a growing city," warned Congressman Charles L. Weltner of Atlanta, Georgia, in 1964. "There is a type of Parkinson's Law working here. 'One more lane of expressway will produce twice as many cars as it can handle.' "

Weltner had introduced a bill to provide federal funds to help cities "develop alternatives to expressways, traffic jams, parking lots and carbon monoxide," but nine years and three Presidents later, when Angelenos were still driving to work in their individual smog factories, the Secretary of Transportation reminded them that although federal money was available in his department for cities to plan and build rapid transit systems, none of it seemed to be going to Los Angeles.

"I have not seen an application yet," he said, dismayed by the sight of so many millions of automobile addicts who "don't know how to break the habit."

✳　✳　✳

Angelenos, in the 1950's, debated the desirability of building backyard air raid shelters, read *Peyton Place*, sang *Three Coins in the Fountain*, watched the Kefauver and McCarthy hearings on television, survived the hula hoop craze, quoted the latest quips of Mort Sahl and Lenny Bruce, detected the scent of marijuana floating above the beatnik pads of Venice, prevented Premier Khrushchev from visiting Disneyland and squinted at the evening sky, trying to catch a glimpse of the Russian satellite orbiting the earth.

The day most likely to remain fixed in middle-aged memories of the decade, however, is October 1, 1957 (three days before Russian scientists launched Sputnik I), when the county's 5,500,-000 inhabitants were required, under penalty of a $500 fine and a 6-month prison term, to abandon their incinerators in favor of

116

trash cans, one of which had to be set aside for non-combustible rubbish.

The switch paved the way for Mayor Yorty's desegregation of tin cans and table scraps, and, although it was not visible to the naked, smog-reddened eye, it also reduced dustfall in the city's air to about the 1940 level. Of even more significance, it bore out A. J. Haagen-Smit's discovery that the chief offender in polluting the air was the automobile.

"In 1940 there were about 1,200,000 vehicles in the Los Angeles area," Dr. Haagen-Smit wrote in *Scientific American* (January, 1964); "in 1950 there were 2,000,000; today there are 3,500,-000. These vehicles burn about 7,000,000 gallons or 21,500 tons, of gasoline a day. They emit 1,800 tons of unburned hydrocarbons, 500 tons of oxides of nitrogen and 9,000 tons of carbon monoxide a day. These emissions outweigh those from all other sources."

✳ ✳ ✳

"The most American of all American cities," Hamilton Basso decided when he visited Los Angeles on an assignment for *Holiday* (January, 1950), and, with a slight shudder, took note of "a growing school of thought that it might very well be on its way to becoming the greatest of all American cities."

Basso marvelled at its newness ("most of what is now Los Angeles—seven-eighths of it, to be exact—has grown up in the past thirty years"). He looked in on the Sunset Strip, dined at Chasen's and Romanoff's, visited the harbor, noted the deficiencies of the local transportation system ("can't even begin to meet the demands placed on it") and paid a ceremonial visit to Forest Lawn ("a country club for the dead").

Once he had sorted out his notes and impressions, he added up the city's faults and virtues ("its belief in newness and bigness, its addiction to fads, its hope for the future, its willingness to try anything once, its idealistic pragmatism, its cultural gropings and materialistic grain") and came to the conclusion that he was looking at "our national character writ large."

The diagnosticians who, like Mr. Basso, dropped by from time to time to see what the inmates were up to in the country's largest open-air asylum generally came from New York, a city swollen by quite a different stream of immigration. The New York melting pot had boiled and bubbled for generations with huddled masses of Europeans yearning to breathe free. Southern California, on the other hand, had been overrun by shivering midwesterners aching to warm their arthritic joints in the winter sun.

The Europeans had come to the New World with empty pockets to build a new life. The midwesterners had come to the New Eden with the profit they'd turned by selling the farm or the feed store, enough to tide them over until they died with a healthy tan. In New York, the emigres had sought to better their lot in life by joining a labor union and the Democratic Party. In Los Angeles, the newcomers looked to the Republican Party, the Protestant ministry and the open-shop *Los Angeles Times* to see that their savings and their way of life were protected from welfare chiselers, Communists and One Worlders.

Some 50,000 Southern California Iowans showed up at a state picnic in 1950 and Governor Warren was there to shake them by the hand. Twenty years later the *Times* had stopped covering the affairs and governors no longer came to share the old folks' fried chicken and potato salad, but the political, social and cultural life of the region was permeated by their fears of a world teeming with young, drug-crazed, free-loving disbelievers who had turned their backs on home, church, flag and Ivory soap.

"Down through the years," Bruce Bliven wrote in *The Reporter* (January 18, 1962), "California conservatives have experienced a series of alarms special to that state. While some of the poorest embraced the Townsend Plan and other fantastic schemes for unearned old-age pensions, many more were frightened by them. Some elderly people are still shaking from Upton Sinclair's campaign for Governor in 1934, with its radical proposals for state aid to the unemployed. Public-opinion polls showed he had formidable strength until late in the campaign; then movie newsreels suddenly appeared in all the theaters showing repulsive tramps—who strikingly resembled well made-up actors from Central Casting—crawling out of boxcars in the Los Angeles yards and announcing happily and with admirable diction to the sound cameras, which just happened to be there, that they had come to share the wealth with Uppie. He was defeated."

In the transitional months between the regimes of Dwight Eisenhower and John Kennedy, when the White House passed into the hands of the first President to be born in the 20th Century, elderly Angelenos rooted in the past and fearful of the future fell in behind a new defender of the faith, a wealthy candy-maker who had come up with the remarkable notion that, unbeknownst to his millionaire golf cronies and the American electorate as well, President Eisenhower was "a dedicated, conscious agent of the Communist conspiracy."

"Subversion, whether of the left or right, is still subversion," thundered the *Times* in 1961, after publication of Gene Blake's series of articles on the John Birch Society prompted thousands of lifelong readers to cancel their subscriptions. The series served notice on what the paper likes to call the Southland that a new generation, represented by General Otis's great-grandson, Otis Chandler (Stanford, Class of '50), had taken command at First and Spring. If there were any doubts at the California Club, they were dispelled three years later when the editorial page suddenly bristled with the political cartoons of Paul Conrad.

✳ ✳ ✳

"Los Angeles is sweeping into high gear this year on a $101,-179,805 expansion of the Civic Center," Ray Zeman reported in the *Times* as the 1960's opened, and rattled off a list of new public buildings designed to shelter peace officers, judges, law librarians, public health officials and a mind-curdling assortment of city, county, state and federal bureaucrats. Meanwhile, the Civic Center was being ringed by freeways. "Its northwest corner—Sunset Boulevard and Figueroa Street—will be a four-level cloverleaf and already ranks as the busiest automobile intersection in the world."

In less than three years after the successful launching of Sputnik, Southern California had become the nation's electronics capital and, before the 1970's ended, Richard B. Leng, vice president of Western Electronic Manufacturers' Association, predicted, "man may even reach the moon," but a dark planetary cloud hung over the new decade, an astrologer warned Hedda Hopper's readers on New Year's Day, 1960.

"Whenever Saturn conjuncts with Jupiter in Capricorn, an earth sign, it has a strong influence in world affairs," Blanca Holmes pointed out, and went on to explain that in astrological circles it was axiomatic that "no President going into office under the shadow of this conjunction . . . ever lives through his elected term of office."

Next day Senator John F. Kennedy announced his decision to seek the Democratic Party's nomination for President. He flew to Los Angeles in July to claim the victory he had won in the primaries of Wisconsin and West Virginia. The convention got off to an unfortunate start when the chairman of the committee that had selected Los Angeles was met at International Airport by two lawmen who tossed him in the Venice drunk tank. Then a workman at the Sports Arena discovered that the four caucus rooms under the podium had been bugged.

Delegates complained about the risks they ran in driving the city's freeways and the fares they paid to travel by cab. It cost a Pennsylvanian, sheltered in Pasadena, $15 to ride over to the midtown Los Angeles digs assigned to New Yorkers. But the natives were friendly and the relentless torrents of rhetoric were relieved by the sight of Golden Girls nipping about the Sports Arena in candy-striped dresses. The convention turned out to be the most abstemious in the party's history. When the last cliche had sounded, janitors tidied up the place and found only ten empty whisky bottles. ✳ ✳ ✳

Angelenos roared with rage in the summer of 1961, when a Las Vegas civil defense official disclosed plans for a 5,000-man militia to repulse Southern Californians who, in the event of a thermonuclear attack, could be expected to "come in like a swarm of human locusts, and pick the valley clean of food, medical supplies and other goods."

While Nevada officials were taking steps to defend the state's resources against a wartime invasion of its neighbors, a parcel of private citizens on the other side of the border, alarmed by the daily influx of 1,600 new Californians, was trying to awaken public officials to the need to husband the state's resources. These peacetime locusts were swarming over a deteriorating paradise dotted with what the founding fathers of California Tomorrow called "slurbs," a word they defined as "sloppy, sleazy, slovenly, slipshod semi-cities."

"We might have to decide how big a given city should be, in order to sponsor healthy home life, healthy business and industry while protecting agriculture and the beauty of our countryside," the group declared, and Assembly Speaker Jesse Unruh of Los Angeles agreed that "we run the real risk of turning bright and golden California into a smog-ridden, sprawling wasteland of a parking lot, unfit for human habitation and useless to agriculture."

Within a year, however, a gleeful governor was calling on his constituents to join him in a four-day celebration of California's emergence as the country's most populous state. According to the official calculations of the Census Bureau, California overtook New York on July 1, 1964, but Governor Brown, using the projections of his own population experts, insisted the historic event had taken place sometime in the fall of 1962.

"As the momentous shift of population from the Atlantic to the Pacific has come about, we have met it with the vision and determination characteristic of our people," the Governor proclaimed on October 15, 1962.

It would have been a proud and glorious day for General Otis, but his great-grandson's editors, whose children were attending half-day sessions and turning up with respiratory ailments, were having second thoughts about the booster spirit which had deposited more than 6,000,000 people in Los Angeles County, giving it a population larger than that of 44 states.

"The promise and potential of bigness can be lost if the problems it creates are ignored," the paper editorialized, and featured a sobering article by Paul Weeks: "Rampant growth breeds crises that take up permanent abode—traffic strangulation, water shortage, air pollution, school overcrowding, racial pressures, exploding slums, rising crime, overloaded court calendars, overtaxed recreational facilities, fire and flood peril, hospital bed shortages, disrupted family ties in a rootless population."

Watts, a modest working-class community, on the eve of World War I.

*The accumulated anger and frustration of the black ghetto ex-
plode on a hot summer night—August 11, 1965.*

"After 25 years of haphazard growth and unprecedented prosperity, Los Angeles now faces the same tough economic and social problems that confronted older cities years ago," the editors of *U.S. News & World Report* concluded in the summer of 1965, when the flames of Watts made it clear for all to see that "the easy life is coming to an end in the country's third largest city."

$$* \quad * \quad *$$

On the hot summer night of Wednesday, August 11, 1965, two black youths driving home in their mother's 10-year-old Buick were stopped around 7 o'clock by a white California Highway Patrol officer on Avalon Boulevard, just north of 116th Place. A crowd gathered, the officer broadcast a Code 1199 ("Officer Needs Help!") and, after a bit of scuffling and name-calling, the lawmen drove off with the two young men, their mother and a black girl who had come out of a nearby beauty parlor, hair still in curlers, to see what was going on.

The Watts-Willowbrook area exploded. After six days of burning and looting, 34 persons were dead, 1,032 wounded, and 3,952 had been arrested. Property damage was estimated at $40,-000,000. In the flames of Charcoal Alley, white Angelenos caught a glimpse of the pent-up anger and frustration of rural blacks trapped in an urban slum patrolled by white police officers long on zeal and short on sensitivity.

Police Chief William H. Parker bridled at any suggestion that the riot (or, as they called it in Watts, the uprising) had sprung from smoldering resentment of police brutality. Quite the contrary, he insisted, the trouble might never have happened if the police had not been handling Negroes "with kid gloves." The eruption should be attributed to the weather, he insisted. People had simply given vent to their emotions on an uncomfortably warm evening.

"I'd be out of sorts now," the chief told reporters, "if I didn't have air conditioning."

Blacks in Los Angeles had been making do not only without air conditioning, but also without jobs, education, decent housing, adequate medical care, parks and public transportation. Five years after the embers of Watts had cooled, unemployment in Los Angeles had gone down to 4.3 per cent, but among blacks it had shot up to 16 per cent. While middle-class homeowners in the San Fernando Valley (96 per cent white) were driving to work on the state's multi-million-dollar freeways, unemployed blacks were still dependent on the outdated bus system of a mobile megalopolis where to be without a car is to be crippled.

✳   ✳   ✳

Ironically, black Angelenos and their Chicano neighbors have been isolated by whites in a city founded by black and brown colonists. Young Chicanos see reminders of their heritage in streets named for their forebears and in the tourist attraction Anglos have made of the Plaza, but black children are left in ignorance of their heritage. Few ever learn that the San Fernando Valley and Beverly Hills were once owned by blacks; that Pio Pico, the last of the Mexican governors of California, had a grandmother listed by census-takers as a *mulata;* and that one of the first two Americans to settle in Los Angeles was a black man named Thomas Fisher, who came ashore from a pirate ship in 1818.

In the years preceding the Civil War, a black barber, Peter Biggs, was much in evidence along Main Street, where he figured in a rich body of anecdote. Georgia-born Biddy Mason came to California as a slave in 1851, won her freedom in court, went to work for a white doctor, put her savings in real estate and built a home at 331 South Spring Street known to every Angeleno down on his luck. The softest touch in town, Mrs. Mason once left word with a grocery store to give flood victims whatever they needed and put it on her tab.

On February 12, 1909, taking note of the one hundredth anniversary of Abraham Lincoln's birth, the *Times* published a supplement devoted to the city's black community. Its leading capitalist was Biddy Mason's grandson, Robert C. Owens, who, with his brother, Henry, had once run a stable on the family's Spring Street property. Like his grandmother, he had also dabbled in real estate. A lot on Hill Street between Seventh and Eighth, bought in 1890 for $7,200, had sold in 1905 for $75,000. As for the family's Spring Street property, the paper pointed out, it "could not be bought for a quarter of a million dollars."

Between 1910 and 1920 the number of black Angelenos more than doubled, jumping from 7,599 to 15,579, but they still made up only 2.7 per cent of the city's total population. In the 1920's their ranks again doubled and the city's whites kept them isolated by housing covenants. They were permitted to swim in public pools only on Thursdays, the day before the water was changed.

In 1934, when blacks were competing with whites for non-existent jobs and the city was undergoing one of its intermittent Red scares, Chief of Police James E. Davis drove over to Pasadena to share his expertise on Communism with his colleagues at the annual convention of the state's peace officers.

"Here in Los Angeles," the chief said, "to practically demonstrate that under Communism pigmentation of skin makes no difference, quite a number of white Communist females are living with Negroes. And that is having a tremendous psychological effect among the blacks not alone of Los Angeles but throughout the nation, where that national program of living with Negroes is practiced by Communist girls. So that the twelve or fifteen million of those Negroes living in America can see that the last great prejudice retained by any people that are white against the blacks is that of living together, and that prejudice cannot exist under Communism. So that tremendous progress is being made with that racial group."

Horace R. Cayton, co-author of *Black Metropolis*, looked in on the postwar city and found it "overcrowded, tense and tawdry," but "most of the middle class and upper class Negroes, as well as a good number of just common folk, have purchased attractive private dwellings in nice, quiet neighborhoods." He was taken aback by the ardor with which white Angelenos enforced restrictive covenants ("they even use them against American Indians"), but, he reported in *Negro Digest* (October, 1947), "people up and down Central Avenue seem very happy...."

During the 1950's the number of blacks in the city rose from 171,209 to 334,916, but despite the 1948 Supreme Court decision outlawing racial covenants, whites had been so successful in keeping them out of their neighborhoods that in 1960 only 21,050 lived outside the city's central district. Even when families moved away, they were likely to end up in the black ghettos of San Pedro, Venice and Pacoima.

"This is the most segregated city I've ever known," a black businessman from the South said in the summer of 1962, three years before Watts.

Back in 1904, when two black Angelenos went to court to protest discrimination by the Grand Opera House, their lawyer, F. W. Allender, suggested that the time had come "for the citizens of this city to settle the matter of which laws they will obey. If the Mississippi plan of having one law for white people and one for Negroes is to obtain, we should know it now. However, we do not believe public sentiment in this city will tolerate the heathenism practiced upon law-abiding Negroes in Mississippi and in other states."

Two generations later, when children went back to school at the start of the 1970-71 term, fifteen years had passed since the Supreme Court's ruling against racially segregated schools, but while more than 26 per cent of Mississippi's black children and nearly 45 per cent of South Carolina's were attending predominantly white schools, only 6 per cent of the 155,000 black schoolchildren of Los Angeles were going to school in the city's white enclaves.

* * *

Chicanos drop out of school a year or two earlier than their black contemporaries. Like the black children, they are born into a world where houses are falling apart, food is scarce, jobs hard to come by, streets ridden with crime and classrooms overcrowded, but the young Mexican-American runs up against the additional barrier of speaking a foreign language in the land of his ancestors.

"You know it from the beginning: speaking Spanish makes you different," Ruben Salazar wrote in *Stranger in One's Land*. "Your mother, father, brothers, sisters, and friends all speak Spanish. But the bus driver, the teacher, the policeman, the store clerk, the man who comes to collect the rent—all the people who are doing the important things—do not. Then the day comes when your teacher

—who has taught you the importance of many things—tells you that speaking Spanish is wrong...."

"The Chicano is completely lost in this society," Sydney Reibscheid of the *Los Angeles Daily Journal* was told in the summer of 1972 when she interviewed Legal Aid Community Representative Eduardo Ruiz. "Even though he lives in the American society, he is completely outside of it. He has Spanish television stations and Spanish stores. In reality, he doesn't even have to read the English language in order to get along. The only time he needs it is when he goes to buy a refrigerator or a television. And then if he only knows Spanish, he will be charged double price."

The Spanish-surname population of the Los Angeles metropolitan area was 1,289,311 in the 1970 census figures released in the spring of 1972, but the barrios had been so effectively gerrymandered into a state of political impotence that Chicanos had only one member of Congress, no State Senators, four Assemblymen and no representation on the Board of Supervisors or the City Council.

For years the Spanish-speaking families of the Ninth Councilmanic District had been represented in City Hall by their political *Papacito*, Edward Roybal. When he was elected to Congress in 1962, the City Council was feuding with the Mayor, as usual, and to assert its independence, it took the seat away from a Chicano candidate in Yorty's office (he also happened to be a cousin of Roybal's) and gave it to Supervisor Kenneth Hahn's 62-year-old black field deputy, Gilbert Lindsay.

In 1964, when councilmanic districts were redrawn to conform with the Supreme Court's reapportionment rulings, Councilman Lindsay got the downtown area, thus acquiring a pride of corporate constituents who have contributed generously to his reelection campaigns. In the meantime, two other blacks, Billy Mills and Thomas Bradley, had been elected to the City Council, but none of its fifteen members in the early 1970's was of Mexican descent.

"Unlike the Negroes, the second largest minority in California, Mexican-Americans have no real political cohesion," Ruben Salazar pointed out in 1963, and cited the 1961 effort to incorporate

128

East Los Angeles. Less than half of the barrio's voters (46 per cent) had bothered to go to the polls. Incorporation lost by 340 votes. Another effort failed in 1964 because of insufficient signatures on petitions.*

On August 29, 1970, five years after the Watts explosion, violence erupted in East Los Angeles, and one of its victims was Ruben Salazar who was killed by a tear gas missile fired into the Silver Dollar Cafe on Whittier Boulevard by a member of the Sheriff's department. A year later, community leaders agreed, the barrio still faced the same basic problems—unemployment, poor housing, inadequate educational opportunities, lack of political representation and strained relations with the police.

"I sometimes feel that out of the ashes just came more ashes," said Richard Martinez, president of the Congress of Mexican-American Unity.

* * *

"I grew up under the system that said you can't do this, you can't go there, you cannot achieve this position," recalled Councilman Tom Bradley, son of a black sharecropper, when he took his second campaign against Mayor Yorty to the Los Angeles campus of the University of California in the spring of 1973.

For many young people in the audience, Bradley's experience four years earlier had demonstrated that the system was still operative. Black Angelenos might be swimming in public pools and serving on the City Council, but white Angelenos had drawn the line at entrusting City Hall to a black mayor. In the primary, three out of four voters had indicated a desire to restore Sam Yorty to private life, but in the general election they had kept him in office simply because his opponent was black.

After his predicted victory of 1969 had vanished beneath an avalanche of votes from the white precincts of the San Fernando Valley, Bradley spoke to his campaign workers, many of whom were young and, at the moment, disillusioned.

"We have tried to prove that the democratic process can work,"

*A fresh proposal to incorporate the 6.64-square-mile area was made to the county, April 19, 1973. If successful, the Mexican-American city would have a population of 86,490, with 26,060 registered voters, 23,576 dwelling units and an assessed valuation of $124,308,285.

he said. "Never give up that hope. I have lived by that belief all my life, and I will not give up now."

Next day he started his 1973 campaign. On the surface it appeared to be a replay of the earlier race. Again Yorty was turned down by a majority of the city's voters in the primary and again he counted on winning the runoff with racial slurs and innunedos designed to link his mild-mannered, moderately liberal challenger with black bomb-throwers, but this time it didn't work.

As the landslide rolled over him on election night, Yorty refused to make the traditional concession speech or send a congratulatory telegram to the mayor-elect. Instead, he turned angrily on his Valley neighbors, blaming them for the defeat he refused, at that hour, to acknowledge.

"The change, if it takes place, will be a very radical one," he predicted, and warned his negligent followers that they would wish they had gone out to vote.

Change was, of course, inevitable and possibly radical, but not in the sense of the Mayor's implied threat of black gangs prowling the streets of Sherman Oaks, while Bradley's black appointees in City Hall reenacted scenes from *The Birth of a Nation*. What seemed more likely was a radical new working relationship between the Mayor and the City Council, a radical overhauling of the city's discredited commissions, and the radical innovation of a Los Angeles mayor appearing before the Board of Education to fight for the city's children and flying to Sacramento and Washington to fight for a rail rapid transit system.

"For twelve years," Bill Boyarsky wrote in the *Times* the day after the election, "the same men have run the mayoral administration, guiding the city along lines favorable to the unrestricted growth that has characterized the Los Angeles Basin for decades. Bradley has said the era of unrestricted growth has ended, that the city must now pay more attention to the quality of life."

· VIII ·
Present Indicative, the 1970's

*"I love the way the buildings are tall and modern and ancient.
And I love all the people, all of them, no two alike . . . I love
the traffic when you can look at the other people and wonder
where they're all headed. And in Los Angeles you never
feel weird, or out of place. . . ."—Maria Matlove, a senior at
El Monte High School, in a letter to Jack Smith, 1973.*

The Central City's new skyline towers above the universal problems of congestion, pollution, poverty and lawlessness, none of which is new to the pueblo. Main Street in 1910 was described by the *Times* as a mixture of "skyscrapers and hovels." Young hoodlums were stealing buggy whips in the 1880's and hubcaps in the 1970's. A Los Angeles banker, in 1930, unburdened himself of the thought: "Modern criminals do not seem to have any fear of the law. A mistaken leniency on the part of many judges has much to do with this."

Sheriff Peter J. Pitchess, in 1972, defied the National Rifle Association by supporting a proposal to outlaw handguns. "Our society is experiencing catastrophic upheaval," he told a Congressional subcommittee. "Our attitudes must change to conform to the demands of contemporary cultures," Under a two-column headline, POLICE PLAN TO LIST ALL SHOOTING IRONS, the *Times* reported on June 13, 1908 that the city's acting chief of police had instituted "a sweeping crusade against the promiscuous sale of firearms."

California lawmakers are currently looking into the feasibility of easing the taxpayer's burden without destroying his moral fibers by legalizing gambling in a state where churches are not permitted to play bingo, but their communicants are free to blow their rent money at a racetrack. One hundred and thirty years ago, in June 1841, the Governor of California dropped a note to the prefect of Angeles, as the Southern California *ciudad* was commonly called, "desiring that some persons of the city shall propose regulations for horse races, so that the municipal funds may receive some benefit from a tax thereon."

Air pollution is regarded as a disagreeable by-product of modern technology, with the gaseous exhalations of the internal combustion engine singled out for the heaviest share of the blame, but in 1877, before Angelenos had seen their first bicycle, much less their first horseless carriage, a City Council committee, choking on the dust swirling up from the unpaved streets of the business district, warned that air pollution in downtown Los Angeles was so bad "it does not allow invalids with lung disease to remain here."

* * *

From his office at Twentieth Century-Fox Film Corporation ("Here I am, back in the Industry for a spell, but thinking of another historical study for later on"), Aldous Huxley dropped a note to his bookseller friend, Jake Zeitlin, in the summer of 1961, asking for some books relating to "the case of the diabolic possessions at Loudun, during the seventeenth century." In an aside, he conveyed his gratitude to Mrs. Zeitlin for having sent him a copy of a book he mistakenly referred to as *Prelude to a Master Plan*.

"I suppose the trouble will be that the prelude is not likely at any near date to be followed by the plan, and that while they're thinking about it, Los Angeles will grow out of all recognition and the problem become even more difficult and costly to solve than it is at present," Huxley wrote in the erroneous belief that the book had just come out. Actually, twenty years had gone by since publication of *Los Angeles: Preface to a Master Plan*, edited by George W. Robbins and L. Deming Tilton.

Clarence Dykstra, in the book's introductory essay, had referred to Los Angeles as a boastful, adolescent city which, because of "its size, rapid growth, and the serious nature of its problems," should recognize the compelling need for "a vigorous, well-supported comprehensive study of its future, its prospects, its potentialities, its limitations, and organic problems."

Thirty years after Dykstra wrote his essay, the city's Planning Department had more professional planners on its staff than any other American city of record, but it still had no master plan and, as Huxley had foreseen, the problem of its uncontrolled growth had, indeed, become "more difficult and costly to solve."

"Recognizing and facing reality is fundamental to planning," says Professor Melville C. Branch, who served for nine years (1961-70) as the City Planning Commission's lone professional planner. "It is not innately easy for people to forego present needs and desires for future benefits which they may not even enjoy because they will accrue to the next generation."

* * *

The next generation (along with the future value of downtown real estate) was in the minds of local businessmen and politicians in the fall of 1970 when the Committee For Central City Planning called on the Philadelphia firm, Wallace, McHarg, Roberts & Todd to prepare a plan to revitalize the downtown area. It was unveiled at the Music Center on a sparkling spring morning in 1972, and on at least one point there was general agreement. John Pastier stated it in the *Times*.

"The plan is, realistically speaking, the last chance to prevent major problems."

Under the Philadelphia plan, some 350 Central City blocks in varying stages of decay would be declared an urban renewal district. The derelicts of Skid Row would be sobered up and straightened out, and their soup kitchens would give way to a new central public library and a university complex. A 125-acre produce distribution center would dominate an east-side industrial park. In the southwest area, an "urban village" would be built around a park and an 80-acre lake designed to provide a peaceful oasis for young couples on the way up and elderly relicts on the way out.

"Urban centers will continue to grow or they will stagnate," said William J. Bird, chairman of the Committee for Central City Planning, referring specifically to the need to "grow in size." Some weeks earlier, in an interview with *Times* columnist Art Seidenbaum, one of the architects of the Philadelphia plan had pointed out that Los Angeles was "still wedded to the growth philosophy," but he had used "growth" in the sense of change, not size ("To grow is to live, to stop growing is to die").

If downtown Los Angeles is to be restored to its historic eminence as the region's commercial and cultural center, if it is to be made into an agreeable place where people can live, work, play, shop, dine, confront their government and rear their young, the city fathers will have to start work—and start at once, warn the Philadelphia planners—on a regional mass rapid transit system.

But a year after the press and public were given their first look at the Central City plan, it lay deep in the bureaucratic backwaters of City Hall and Angelenos were no closer to a mass rapid transit system than they had been a generation earlier when Richard Sachse, a consulting engineer, had wondered "why in our day a distinction is made, from the point of view of public need, between a system of public streets and a system of public transportation operating upon such streets. Both serve the same end and purpose exactly."

* * *

Now that the boulevards of the earth's major cities are all clogged with motorists crawling through the same noxious haze in search of a place to park, it has become the journalistic fashion to dub Los Angeles "the ultimate city" or "the prototype of supercity." The same idea occurred to Bruce Bliven in 1927, when he referred to the booming metropolis as "a melting-pot in which the civilization of the future may be seen bubbling darkly up in a foreshadowing brew."

"Here the future's present tense," wrote the songwriting team of Jay Livingston and Ray Evans in *Angeltown* (1959). A current cliche paraphrases Lincoln Steffens' remark on his return from the Soviet Union in 1919: "I have seen the future, and it doesn't work."*

By rights, no metropolis of such magnitude should have sprung up on the Yangna villagers' hunting grounds, but Angelenos have always managed to do the unexpected. The founding fathers grew more grain than anyone had thought possible. Their successors proceeded to raise more cattle, press more wine, ship more oranges, pump more oil, pick more flowers and build more fighter-bombers than even the most ebullient prophets had foreseen.

"Life in Los Angeles is a tonic," the *Times* chirped in 1906, when it was rounding out its twenty-fifth year. "Optimism, hopefulness, and courage are in the air. As one comes downtown in the morning one feels ready for the day's battle, like a giant refreshed with new wine."

The giant, in each generation, has kicked aside the pueblo's past to make way for its future. Street-builders in the 1880's casually destroyed the site of Fort Moore. Fifty years later the historic hill was chewed up for a continuation of Spring Street. The dirt was hauled a few blocks away to improve the approaches to the new Union Passenger Terminal and, in the process, bury old Chinatown.

"Those lots on Bunker Hill will double in value in one year," the *Star* predicted in 1874, when Prudent Beaudry carved out the city's first hillside subdivision.

As the city moved west toward the sea, men who had grown old and rich buying and selling, lending and speculating, healing and suing, abandoned Bunker Hill to fling up French chateaux and English manor houses on the recycled beanfields of Beverly Hills. The Gothic mansions of their childhood were left to a mixed lot of pensioners, prostitutes and petty criminals.

"In the tall rooms haggard landladies bicker with shifty tenants," Raymond Chandler wrote in *The High Window* (1942).

*His actual words were, "I have been over into the future, and it works."

135

Bunker Hill, as Raymond Chandler saw its fading elegance in the 1940's.

The performing arts find a home on a hill in the 1960's.

"On the wide cool front porches, reaching their cracked shoes into the sun, and staring at nothing, sit the old men with faces like lost battles."

In the last twenty years both the faded 19th century elegance and the unwanted 20th century decay have been pushed aside to provide high-rise accommodations ("You can live above it all at the Bunker Hill Towers") within walking distance of the city's center for the performing arts, the West's financial heartland and the country's most massive congeries of government buildings this side of the Potomac.

West-end burghers who in the old days would have lived long and possibly useful lines without ever setting foot in downtown Los Angeles except to answer a jury summons are now dining at the Pavilion or the Tower before taking in a play or a concert at the Music Center. An earlier generation would have eaten at Good Fellow's Grotto on South Main Street before going on to the Belasco or the Hippodrome. When it closed in December, 1953, Good Fellow's was the city's oldest restaurant. It was forty-eight.

"I find a city flush with enthusiastic life and filled to the brim with business," a visitor wrote the editor of the *News* in 1867, and a generation later, reading a paper to a klatch of county pioneers in 1905, a local antiquarian declared: "The new Los Angeles is one of the most unique cities of modern times."

It is still flush with enthusiastic life, still filled to the brim with business, still new, still unique (where else do young couples pass funeral processions on their way to the cemetery to get married?) and still erasing yesterday's landmarks to run up full-scale models of tomorrow's megalopolis. In view of the odds against the pueblo at the outset (can eleven illiterate families with twenty-two children find happiness in a heathen wilderness?), there seems to be a sporting chance that the future may work.

Los Angeles Miscellany

ANGELS FLIGHT

On grand opening day, New Year's Eve, 1901, passengers got a free ride and a dollop of fruit punch. The Third and Hill Street landmark was dismantled in the spring of 1969. Its two orange-and-black cars, Olivet and Sinai, are preserved at the Heritage Museum, 1200 Olive St. Angels Flight was not the city's first cable car line. That distinction belongs to the Second Street Cable Railroad, which on October 8, 1885 made its pre-opening trial run, using a dummy.

AREA

Under the terms of its Spanish land grant of 1781, El Pueblo's original area was four square leagues (28 square miles), but when the city hired an attorney to appear before the United States Land Commission in the 1850's to confirm its title to the pueblo lands, he applied for an area four leagues square, which would have given his client a royal legacy of sixteen square leagues (162 square miles). He settled for four. The city's physical growth was stunted until 1895 when it took off on an annexation spree which began with Highland Park. It added the sober, God-fearing community of Hollywood in 1910 and a chunk of the San Fernando Valley five years later. The city's 315-mile boundaries now encompass an area of 463.7 square miles.

AUTOMOBILES

In the early morning hours of Sunday, May 30, 1897, J. Philip Erie bundled his wife and half a dozen friends into a four-cylinder, gasoline-powered horseless carriage he and S. D. Sturgis had put together in a West Fifth Street shop at a cost of $30,000. "This innocent-looking black tally-ho has about twenty-five miles an hour concealed in its vitals," the *Times* reported next day, and went on to predict that it would "not be long before a factory is established in Los Angeles for the manufacture of motor wagons." By 1915, with 55,217 cars distributed among its 750,000 inhabitants, Los Angeles County led the world in the ownership of automobiles. It still does.

AVIATION

On January 10, 1910, at the opening of the country's first international air meet, Glenn H. Curtiss piloted the first airplane to make a successful flight on the Pacific Coast. On the final day of the meet, January 20, Louis Paulhan of France set a world altitude record (4,165 feet). Meanwhile, Lieutenant Paul W. Beck had piqued the interest of the world's war offices by aiming sandbags at a ground target to test the feasibility of airplane bombing.

BANKS

"We have now emerged from a country town to an inland city," the *Los Angeles News* noted on January 10, 1868, when a steamer from San Francisco arrived at San Pedro with iron for the vault of the city's first bank, James A. Hayward & Co. Some months later, on September 1, Isias W. Hellman, F. P. F. Temple and William Workman opened a Main Street bank "with fire-proof iron front," which evolved into Farmers & Merchants National Bank. It merged in 1956 with Security-First National. Around the turn of the century, banking moved west from Main to Spring Street, which in an earlier day had served as the stable entrance for Main Street mansions.

BICYCLES

The first recorded tryout of a velocipede occurred on April 25, 1869 when a carriage-maker's apprentice took a tumble at the junction of Main and Spring Streets. By 1883 wheelmen were careening about the streets at such a clip that pedestrians called on the City Council to draft an ordinance requiring them to install bells and lights as warning devices.

BEER

Lager beer was brought down from San Francisco in 1853 and produced locally the following year. The National Prohibition Amendment took effect on January 16, 1920 and for the next thirteen years Los Angeles was the country's only major dry city outside the South. Legal beer began to flow again April 7, 1933.

Prohibition remained in effect at the Coliseum, however, until the night of December 13, 1971.

BLACKS

Although more than half of the pueblo's founders were of African descent, only a dozen blacks showed up in the 1850 census and only one, the barber Peter Biggs, was given a full name. The rest were recorded simply as William, Clarissa, Julia, Malvina, etc. A half-century later there were 2,131 blacks, accounting for two percent of the city's population. Between 1930 and 1970 their ranks rose from 38,894 (3.1 percent) to 503,606 (17.9 percent). Impoverished black communities are considerably younger than affluent white enclaves. The median age in Watts (91.2 percent black) is 17.18; in Bel-Air (96.5 percent white) it is 39.65.

BRADBURY BUILDING

In the early 1890's, having made a fortune mining in Mexico, Louis Bradbury decided to run up a monument to himself in the form of a downtown office building. Disappointed in the plans of Sumner P. Hunt, a leading Los Angeles architect, he offered the assignment to a young draftsman in Hunt's office, George Herbert Wyman, who had no formal education in architecture. He turned the job down, but one Saturday evening when he and his wife were huddled over a planchette board (a forerunner of the Ouija board), Wyman picked up a message from his dead brother: "Take Bradbury Building. It will make you famous." Eighty years after its completion, architects still make pilgrimages to Third and Broadway to enjoy its inner court bathed in sunlight and to admire its bird-cage elevators, marble paneling, Mexican floor tiles and delicate ironwork. Nothing in the heart of the pueblo is so ageless and joyful. Shortly after he finished work on the building in 1893, Wyman signed up for a correspondence course in architecture and created no more masterpieces.

CATHOLICS

Of the country's 48,460,427 Roman Catholics (1973), 1,875,500 live in the Los Angeles archdiocese, the third largest of the seven in the United States. Chicago, with 2,489,320, ranks first, and Boston, with 1,900,023, second.

CEMETERY

The pueblo's first cemetery serves as a parking lot for the county's venerable Brunswig Building, 513 North Main Street, next door to the Plaza Church. Apparently the more socially prominent remains were removed before the land was reconsecrated to the use of the automobile.

CHICANOS

The county's 1,289,311 Spanish-surname residents account for 18 per cent of its population and, according to 1970 census data, their median income is $8,397 a year, compared with $10,970 for the area as a whole. Of the adults (25 or older), three out of four have spent less than twelve years in school. Of those who were working or looking for a job, 27 per cent were blue-collar workers. One of the conspicuous posters on East Los Angeles walls these days quotes Zapata: "It is better to die on my feet than to continue to live on my knees."

CHINESE

In his memoirs, Harris Newmark labored under the mistaken notion that his Uncle Joseph, in 1854, brought the first Chinese to Los Angeles. He was unaware of the two young men, Ahfou and Alluce, who had turned up in the 1850 census. In 1970 census-takers counted nearly 41,000 Chinese in the metropolitan area. Chinatown has some forty restaurants, the bulwark of its economy and a source of discontent among the young, who would like to see the community offer them something more than washing dishes, selling curios, making noodles or sewing piecework in a garment factory.

CITY HALL

An adobe house across the street from today's City Hall sufficed to accommodate both city and county government in 1853. The City Council moved to a two-story brick building at 213 West Second Street in 1884. Four years later it moved again, this time to a red sandstone-and-tile structure on Broadway between Second and Third. Municipal government came back to its old haunts on April 26, 1928 with the dedication of its new $4,800,000 skyscraper City Hall (twenty-eight stories). It had cost $20,000 less than anticipated. The final tab for the City Hall East-Mall South is expected to exceed $40,000,000, a cost override of from $3,000,-000 to $5,000,000.

COLISEUM

When some 25,000 Angelenos assembled at the Coliseum for its first football game, October 6, 1923 (U.S.C. beat Pomona, 23 to 7), they were confident that in building "the biggest stadium in the world," they had, like the Romans, built for the ages, but as the Coliseum entered its fiftieth year, its tenants, the Rams, were suggesting that their landlord rebuild or replace it.

CONVENTION CENTER

"They've torn up so many buildings for freeways, it used to be that when you got downtown there was nowhere to go," Bob Hope commented on July 10, 1971, when the city opened its new Convention and Exhibition Center, where 8,000 delegates with plastic name-tags can be fed at a sitdown dinner. A bust of the Mayor was unveiled in Sam Yorty Hall the following December 15. It had been paid for by "interested citizens."

COUNTY COURTHOUSE

After holding court for a few months in 1850 in a ramshackle adobe, the county rented space at the Bella Union Hotel, situated at about what is now 314 North Main Street. In May, 1861, court convened on the first floor of the building known as "City Hall and Market House," near the northeast corner of the present-day City Hall. On August 8, 1891, a few months after the birth of Earl Warren (March 19) a few blocks away (457 East Turner Street), six Superior Court judges moved into a new red sandstone courthouse on the corner of Temple and Broadway. Chief Justice Warren delivered the dedicatory address on October 31, 1958, when the cornerstone was laid for the present courthouse, sealing such documents as the county's business license ordinance, a statement of bonded indebtedness and the regulations of the Air Pollution Control District.

DRUG STORE

"I will teach them how to take medicine," 23-year-old John G. Downey said in 1850 when an old Los Angeles hand advised against opening a drug store in "the healthiest country in the world." With James P. McFarland as his partner, the personable young Irishman set up shop in a small adobe building on the northwest corner of Los Angeles and Commercial Streets. Three years later, having accumulated $30,000, he began buying up land, including the site of the city which now bears his name.

FIRE DEPARTMENT

In December, 1865, when San Franciscans talked of establishing a paid fire department, the *Los Angeles News* snorted: "By all means pay the firemen one or two hundred dollars per month; the taxpayers of San Francisco are rich and can afford it." A volunteer firefighting force "to consist of not more than three steam fire engine companies" was created by the Los Angeles City Council on December 8, 1871. The firemen were added to the municipal payroll on December 1, 1885. They got $100 a month.

FOREIGNERS

El Pueblo's first foreigner, José Antonio Rocha, arrived from Portugal in 1815 and ran up a pretentious home which was later to serve as the first city hall. The first American Angelenos were two pirates who came ashore in 1818 and promptly mended their ways. One was a black buccaneer, Thomas Fisher, who seems to have vanished among the Forty-niners; the other was a blonde, blue-eyed Bostonian, Joseph Chapman. His home town and the republic its activists had helped bring into being were so remote from his new neighbors that they called him *El Ingles* (The Englishman).

GRIFFITH PARK

Colonel Griffith J. Griffith appeared before the City Council on December 16, 1896 with an unexpected Christmas gift of 3,015 acres, the world's largest city park. It lay outside the corporate limits until 1910. Its present area is 4,063.87 acres, which makes it larger than Beverly Hills (3,646.7 acres).

HALL OF RECORDS

The venerable landmark, built at a cost of $1,063,644, was the seat of county government for half a century (1911-60). Like the Old Red Courthouse on Poundcake Hill, it was originally aligned with New High Street. When the street was obliterated, the Hall of Records was left standing at an odd angle, like a mildly dotty old lady caught in the crush of civic center traffic. In 1938 and again in 1962 the Board of Supervisors looked into the possibility of relocating the 25,000-ton building, but finally gave up the idea and earmarked it for demolition to make way for an underground garage with a landscaped roof. The new Hall of Records was dedicated May 18, 1962. It cost $11,700,000 and may age with grace and dignity, but is not likely to remind anyone of an elderly aunt who has been nipping at the cooking sherry.

ICE

When Wells Fargo & Company opened an express office in Los Angeles in 1857, it was commissioned to bring the city its first shipment of commercial ice. The undertaking proved to be a financial disaster. In the spring of 1868, when a wagon operating from a Main Street depot started daily deliveries of ice brought by steamer from the Truckee River, the *Los Angeles News* hailed it as "another step forward in the progress that is to make us a great city." A few weeks later the editor watched a demonstration of an ice-making machine imported from Paris, France. "What next?" he wondered. Machine-made ice went on sale in the city April 14, 1871.

ICE CREAM

When Matilda Newmark married Maurice Kremer, April 9, 1856, the bride's father served ice cream. It was, so far as Harris Newmark could remember, the first time Angelenos had tasted it. An ice cream salon, using locally manufactured ice, opened on Spring Street in Temple Block in the early spring of 1871.

JAPANESE-AMERICANS

"All persons of Japanese ancestry, both alien and non-alien, will be evacuated . . ." So runs the wording of the Western Defense

Command's directive of May 3, 1942 carrying out President Roosevelt's Executive Order 9066. Thirty years later, while elderly Issei (born in Japan) congregate at the Pioneer Center on the first floor of Little Tokyo's organizational hub at 125 Weller Street and wonder what the world's coming to, their conservative, middle-aged children (the Nisei) and their liberal, third-generation American grandchildren (the Sansei), are working in upstairs offices to protect the constitutional rights that the old folks, with their traditional respect for properly constituted authority, surrendered with dignity but without a fight. Of the estimated 350,000 Japanese-Americans in the continental United States (not counting Hawaii's 250,000), about 100,000 are to be found in the Los Angeles area. They live six to seven years longer than their Caucasian neighbors.

JEWS

The first Jewish services were held in Los Angeles shortly after the arrival of Joseph Newmark in 1854. The city's first synagogue, a brick building on the east side of Fort Street (Broadway), between Second and Third, was dedicated on August 8, 1873. Only Israel and New York City now have more Jews than the half-million who live in Los Angeles.

LIBRARY

"The absence of a place where a cultivated person may go for books of reference or standard library works has been spoken of to our injury abroad," the *Star* noted on December 5, 1872. That night some two hundred Angelenos met at the Merced Theater and formed a library association. "An original letter by Lord Byron is on view at the library room," the *Star* announced the following spring. The ordinance establishing the public library passed the City Council on March 7, 1878. The central library moved to its present home, 630 West Fifth Street, in July 1926. With its sixty-one branches, it now circulates 13,500,000 books a year.

MOTION PICTURES

On May 10, 1909, Hobart Bosworth, a New York actor who refused to let his name be associated with the enterprise, wrote in his diary: "All Saturday and yesterday I acted as leading man before a kinetoscope, a strange but not unpleasant experience." His scene for *In the Power of the Sultan* was filmed in a Chinese laundry on the west side of Olive Street, just north of Eighth. In 1903 the Electric Theater, 262 South Main Street, became what is thought to be the first theater in the country to devote itself exclusively to the showing of moving pictures. The first studio of any lasting significance was opened in 1911 in an abandoned tavern at the corner of Sunset and Gower. It remained in use for the next sixty-one years, until Columbia Pictures moved in with Warner Brothers at Burbank.

MUSIC CENTER

"This is a historic day," Mrs. Norman Chandler said on November 3, 1960, when the Board of Supervisors unanimously adopted a proposal to raise funds from private sources to help build a Music Center on county-owned land bounded by Temple Street, Grand Avenue, First Street and Hope Street. The Dorothy Chandler Pavilion (3,250 seats) was formally opened on December 6, 1964. The Ahmanson Theater (2,100 seats) and the Mark Taper Forum (750 seats) made their debut the week of April 9-15, 1967.

NEWSPAPERS

The city's first newspaper, the *Star*, made its debut May 17, 1851, and after many vicissitudes folded in the early part of 1879. The *Mirror* first appeared on February 1, 1873. Later that year, on October 2, the *Herald* began publication. It created quite a stir as the first Southern California newspaper to be printed by steam presses. The first issue of the *Times* hit the streets on December 4, 1881. The editor hoped the Republican candidates for city council would prevail in the following day's election. They didn't.

OIL

Indians used the basin's deposits of *brea* (the tar was congealed petroleum) to caulk their boats and waterproof their woven baskets. Pioneer Angelenos covered the roofs of their adobes with it to ward off the rain. In 1855 General Andres Pico sold it as a

147

lamp oil and a medicine. The city's first oil boom, 1864-67, was shortlived, but another boom was touched off in November, 1892, when Edward L. Doheny dug a well near Second Street and Glendale Boulevard. On June 23, 1921, a geyser of crude oil shot up from the depths of a Long Beach hill where early-day Angelenos used to signal ships at sea. In the next fifty years the more than 2,400 wells of Signal Hill produced 859,000,000 barrels of oil. The two-square-mile area incorporated in 1924 and elected the state's first woman mayor, Mrs. Jessie Elwin Nelson.

OLVERA STREET

Originally Wine Street, it was renamed for one of its most distinguished residents, Agustin Olvera, the first county judge. Thanks to a posse of influential crusaders rounded up by Mrs. Christine Sterling in 1928, the filthy, decaying alley was refurbished with prison labor. "Each night," Mrs. Sterling wrote in her diary, November 21, 1929, "I pray they will arrest a bricklayer and a plumber." The Mexican *paseo*, with its string of shops, booths and eating places, was thrown open to the public on April 20, 1930. "Happiness," wrote Mrs. Sterling, "lingers here as it did in the old days."

PARKING METERS

In the late spring of 1949, newfangled hitching posts sprang up in North Hollywood along Lankershim Boulevard from Cumston to Hartsook Streets. On Monday, June 12, police began issuing tickets for motorists who neglected to deposit five cents in the parking meters for a one-hour stay.

PERSHING SQUARE

On December 11, 1866, Mayor Cristobal Aguilar signed an ordinance setting aside five acres of the pueblo's royal land grant as "a Public Square or Plaza, for the use and benefit of the Citizens in common. . . ." It went by various names (Public Square, City Park, Central Park, Sixth Street Park, among others) until November 18, 1918, when the city fathers, caught up in the exuberance of Armistice Day, named it Pershing Square.

PLAZA

The original Plaza was a 200-by-300-foot rectangle northwest of the present-day site. The shift occurred in 1818. "A magnificent ruin," the *Herald* declared in 1874, and in the summer of 1896 the park commissioners were restrained by the city attorney and a group of outraged antiquarians from turning the pueblo's birthplace into a public market. It is now part of a 42-acre park owned by the state and administered by an 11-member commission.

PRETZELS

"Pretzels have made their appearance in Los Angeles," the *Star* announced, June 21, 1871.

PLAZA CHURCH

Although nine miles separated the pueblo's first families from the spiritual resources of Mission San Gabriel, they waited three years before they got around to building a chapel of their own. Another twenty-three years slipped by before they laid the cornerstone of the Nueva Iglesia (New Church) in 1814. The site was flooded the following year and the church moved to higher ground, thus shifting the center of the pueblo. Its Spanish land grant was measured one league (about 2.6 miles) to each wind from the middle of the church door. By the time the church was dedicated on December 8, 1822, Spain's flag had been replaced by the eagle and serpent of the Mexican Empire.

PLAZA DE LA RAZA

For years the recreation center of the East Los Angeles barrio has been Lincoln Park, three miles from the downtown district. In 1969, when local authorities tagged the park's venerable boathouse for demolition, the Chicano community came up with a plan to recycle it. The Plaza de la Raza cultural center is to include administrative offices in the refurbished boathouse, along with the Ruben Salazar Memorial Performing Arts Center, a library, museum and workshops.

POWER POLES

The first pole for the overhead lines of the Bureau of Power and Light was erected in the northeast section of the city at the corner of Pasadena Avenue and Piedmont Street, March 30, 1916. Fifty-five years later the Mayor's Council on Environmental Management, reporting on visual pollution, noted that there were "approximately 6,400 miles of overhead power lines throughout the city."

PRONUNCIATION

"There is no other city in the world whose inhabitants so miserably and shamelessly, and with so many varieties of foolishness, miscall the name of the town they live in," Charles F. Lummis wrote a friend in 1914. He was still shuddering at the memory of hearing Theodore Roosevelt refer to the city as "Loss-AN-gee-lees." Lummis advocated a pronunciation in which "Los" rhymed with "Dose," the A in Angeles was slightly broader than the A in "Arm," the G was hard and the final "es" rhymed with "Yes." He spelled it phonetically: LOCE *ANG*-ELESS.

PROTESTANTS

On a June Sunday in 1850, in a private home near the present site of City Hall, a Methodist minister named J. W. Brier conducted the first Protestant service held in Los Angeles. The first Protestant church was established in 1853 on unhallowed ground where, two years earlier, a pair of army officers had opened a saloon, El Dorado. The two-story structure, made of prefabricated lumber shipped around the Horn from Boston, was the pueblo's first wooden building. When the saloon fell on lean days, the Reverend Adam Bland bought it and converted it to a Methodist Church. It was later razed to clear space for the Merced Theater.

RADIO

"Radiating their voices over the Southwest by the marvel of the wireless and vacuum amplifier of the radiophone, Clifford Lott and Corinne Harris last night entertained with vocal selections," the *Times* reported on April 18, 1922, and began publication of a daily chart indicating "the exact time various stations will be 'on the air.' " A year and a half later, the paper noted, "the radio craze has spread around the globe faster than the influenza."

RAILROADS

The first railroad south of the Tehachapis, the Los Angeles & San Pedro, was formally opened on October 26, 1869 and gobbled up by the Southern Pacific three years later. On September 5, 1876, a golden spike driven into the SP tracks at Lang Station, near Newhall, linked Los Angeles by rail with San Francisco and the east coast. In May 1939, when Angelenos spent three days celebrating the completion of the Union Passenger Terminal, sixty-four trains roared in and out of the city every day. On May 1, 1971, when Amtrak (National Railroad Passenger Corp.), a quasi-governmental operation, took over passenger service for the country's railroads, there were only fifty-two trains a week. But Southern Pacific, "The Octopus" which had once held California politics in its tentacles, remains the state's largest private landowner (2,000,000 acres).

SANTA ANAS

Angelenos are occasionally caressed or battered by a hot, dry wind which has been compared to the *foehn* of the northern Alps and the *hamsin* of the Middle East. Named for the cañon through which they often blow, the Santa Anas occur when air rushes down from the high inland plateaus, sweeps through mountain cañons and bursts suddenly on the lower coastal valleys. Compression heats the air as much as 5.5° for every 1,000 feet of vertical drop, at the same time expelling much of the humidity. The natives are noticeably restless during a Santa Ana. Anything can happen, Raymond Chandler once noted. "Meek little wives feel the edge of the carving knife and study their husbands' necks."

SERVICE STATIONS

Earle C. Anthony, the Los Angeles Packard dealer ("Ask the Man Who Owns One"), toured France in 1912 and, according to William A. Spalding, he "observed that every 100 kilometers or so along main highways there was a sign, 'Petrol,' and that when a car drove up to that sign a man carrying a hose stepped out and pumped as many liters of gasoline into his tank, through the hose, as were ordered . . . That interested him, as then, in this country, it was customary for one to drive into a garage or up to the village grocery and have gasoline poured into the tank from a five-gallon can. On his return home, Anthony told H. L. Arnold what he had seen, and together they worked out an adaptation of the idea. As soon as they could arrange it, they opened, at Grand Avenue and Washington Street, what probably was the first service station in America." The claim provokes an argument in Seattle, where a Standard Oil engineer was dispensing gasoline from a 30-gallon hot water tank as early as 1907.

SMOG
When Juan Rodriguez Cabrillo spotted the brownish haze of Indian fires hanging above the hunting grounds of Southern California, he gave the name *Bahia de los Fumos* (Bay of the Smokes) to what was either the bay of Santa Monica or San Pedro. Four centuries later, on July 27, 1943, under the front-page headline: CITY HUNTING FOR SOURCE OF "GAS ATTACK," the *Times* reported the fourth assault of a "smoke nuisance." A year later, on September 18, a new word passed into the local lexicon when the paper, using an expression common in Pittsburgh, referred to the bronze pall as "smog (smoke and fog)."

STREET LIGHTS
In the pueblo's early days, homeowners on travelled streets were required to hang a lighted lantern in front of their doors on dark nights. A proposal to light the city "by a new process called Aubin gas" was placed before the council in 1857, but not until May 5, 1866 did the city fathers grant a franchise for the erection of a gas works. The councilmen got into an argument with the gas company in 1872 and the company cut off the city's service. Los Angeles claimed to be the first city in the country to be entirely lighted by electricity when its mayor, on New Year's Eve 1882, switched on the current for the new public lighting system. Electric lights, warned gas company propagandists, would cause color blindness and ruin the ladies' complexions.

SUBURBS IN SEARCH OF A CITY

Of all the cliches about El Pueblo, none is more persistent than the designation of Los Angeles as a varying number of suburbs in search of a city. When it cropped up in the London *Daily Telegraph* in the late fall of 1972, Jack Smith suggested in his *Times* column that originally it was "forty suburbs." No one, not even the incomparable Mr. Smith, knows for sure how the thing got started, but the leading authority on such matters, the late W. W. Robinson, was convinced that the phrase dated back to the 1920's when somebody linked the city's urban sprawl with the newly published English translation of Pirandello's play, *Six Characters in Search of an Author.*

TAXICABS

The West's first taxicab, loosed on the city streets on June 16, 1908, by the enterprising Mr. Anthony (see SERVICE STATIONS), proved to be an immediate success. The fare was 30 cents for the first half-mile, 10 cents for each additional quarter-mile. "There is no reason," observed the *Times*, "why a dozen cabs cannot be kept busy here." They still could.

TELEGRAPH

Los Angeles and San Francisco were linked by telegraph October 8, 1860. The first news story sent by wire advised readers of the San Francisco *Bulletin*: "The steamer *Senator* leaves San Pedro tonight with about three thousand boxes of grapes."

TELEPHONES

The Los Angeles Telephone Company, on April 15, 1882, issued its first directory (three pages), instructing users to call the central office ("Ring 'two bells' ") and then "give the telephone number and not the name of the subscriber wanted." Three months later the *Times* reported that the home of the chief of police had just been "connected with the telephone system."

TELEVISION

"For the first time in the United States a regular daily television service using electrical scanning has been effected," announced the Don Lee Broadcasting System following inauguration of its 6-to-7 P.M. broadcasts on December 23, 1931, from radio station KHJ at Seventh and Bixel Streets. The company synchronized radio and television for a weekly series of "sight-sound broadcasts" on September 9, 1936. No television commercials were permitted until July 1, 1941. The industry exploded in Southern California in 1949. The year began with about 80,000 sets and ended with 354,000, most of them tuned in on intercollegiate football games.

THEATER

The city's first English-speaking theater opened July 4, 1848 in an addition to the home of Don Antonio Coronel. William Abbott's Merced Theater was inaugurated December 30, 1870. It shared a common wall with the Pico House, enabling hotel guests to enter and leave the red plush boxes without having to step outside. Abbott was a thin, nervous man, uxorious and ordinarily unshaven. His wife, the formidable Doña Mercedes (née Garcia), and their nine children held down the third floor, while the family breadwinner looked after the theater on the second floor and the furniture store below it. He also moonlighted in the basement as an undertaker.

TRAFFIC LIGHTS

As the city was celebrating the one hundred and fiftieth anniversary of its founding in early September 1931, motorists were getting used to the experimental three-light traffic signals on Wilshire Boulevard between Westlake Park and the west city limits. They were equipped with "a soft-toned gong to signify a change," the *Times* reported, and explained that "the top light is the red 'stop,' the center and amber 'caution' and the bottom one the green 'go.'"

TRAFFIC SIGNS

Boulevard stop signs first appeared at the city's more hazardous intersections in September, 1923, and received a warm welcome from both motorists and pedestrians.

TRANSPORTATION

The city's mass rapid transit system began in September 1873, with two horse-drawn cars which the *Star* described as "splendid and easy-riding omnibuses." The following summer, on July 2, R. M. Widney's Spring and Sixth Street line went into operation. Its owner used it to commute to the office from his country home on Hill Street between Fourth and Fifth. The last horse-drawn streetcar vanished from the city in 1897. On Independence Day, 1902, a crowd of 30,000 turned out to watch a big red car of Henry E. Huntington's Pacific Electric Railway complete the interurban line's first scheduled run to Long Beach. Trolley buffs climbed aboard for the final run on April 8, 1961. Buses were brought in to supplement the local service of the Los Angeles Railway's historic yellow cars on October 10, 1923, but by then more than one-third of city's commuters were driving to work in their own automobiles. The last streetcar retired from service on March 31, 1963. It reached the car barn ten minutes late.

UNION PASSENGER TERMINAL

The city's three major railroads—Southern Pacific, Santa Fe and Union Pacific—should build a common terminal, a planning study recommended in 1911, and six years later the City Council put up $20,000 to look into the proposal. The union station should be built near the Plaza, Angelenos decided at the polls in 1926, but railroad lawyers managed to keep the project tied up in litigation until 1933, when their clients finally agreed to drop the fight. A crowd estimated at half a million showed up to inspect the $11,-000,000 terminal when its massive doors opened on Wednesday, May 3, 1939. The first train pulled in at 6 o'clock the following Sunday morning.

WATER

The founding fathers lost no time in digging a *zanja madre* (mother ditch) to provide water for their fields and for domestic use. The *zanja* system lasted until 1903. Meanwhile, in 1868, the city fathers granted a 30-year monopoly on the distribution of water to a few influential neighbors who had formed a private company. In 1897, as the contract was about to expire, the water company was serving 100,000 Angelenos, but, under the terms of its contract, the City Council was powerless to order a rate reduction below the figures originally set for a town of 15,000. The city acquired the water system for $2,000,000 on February 2, 1902. The Department of Water and Power is now the country's largest municipal utility operation.

WATTS TOWERS

"I had in mind to do something big, and I did," Simon Rodia explained after he'd spent thirty-three years building his three towers (99, 97 and 55 feet high) at 1765 East 107th Street of seashells, tiles, broken bottles and salvaged lengths of iron and steel. When his work was done in 1954, he moved to Martinez, where he died July 17, 1965 without ever having revisited what had come to be regarded as a triumph of twentieth century folk art. In October 1961, two years after bureaucratic vandals in the city's Department of Building and Safety had tried in vain to have the towers torn down (the artist had neglected to take out a building permit), Rodia met with some students at Berkeley. "Do the best you can," he said, when asked what advice he had for young people, "but the way it's going we have so many lawyers we may some day have to get a permit to go to bed."

WEATHER

The *Star's* daily temperature readings were taken from the bookstore thermometer at 13 Spring Street before a U. S. Signal Corps sergeant opened the city's first weather bureau on July 1, 1877. The city's record high, 110°, was established on September 1, 1955; the record low, 27.9°, on January 4, 1949.

YANGNA

The five hundred or so brush huts of Yangna, one of many aboriginal villages in the vicinity, disappeared within fifty years of the pueblo's founding. In 1836 the city's decimated Indian population was crowded into a ghetto near what is now the southeast corner of Commercial and Alameda Streets, an area often mistakenly identified as the original site of Yangna. Its actual location cannot be pinpointed, but was probably within bow and arrow range of present-day City Hall.

Index